I0787189

THE PERCEPTION WARS

How Influence Shapes Conflict

By Alex Hollings

For Jamie and Reagan

Introduction

There has been an explosion in the coverage of foreign influence efforts in the United States in recent years, thanks in large part to the revelation that the Russian government invested a great deal of time and resources into managing the ways Americans perceived the candidates in the 2016 presidential election. However, despite all the discussion, confusion seems to persist regarding how governments work to frame the ways people see the world. Phrases like "hacking the election" are used first as a form of journalistic shorthand, but are soon adopted by the public as a simpler and more digestible abbreviation of what many come to believe the story to be: Russians using computers surreptitiously to manage the outcome of America's election.

The problem is, while the Russian government *did* surreptitiously attempt to exert influence over the American people, and computers were certainly involved, the endeavor in itself was less about *hacking* and more about interaction. Russia's efforts to sow discord among the American populous isn't about them installing spyware or securing passwords -- though elements of Russia's hybrid warfare strategy certainly include those things -- what Russia actually did (and continues to do) is far more nuanced than than that.

In the modern world, and the United States in particular, we've become so inundated with overt messaging through advertising that national level propaganda efforts have been forced to evolve with the populous. Our cynicism toward direct messaging from positions of authority, be it a corporation or government, has led to a more indirect approach to perception management campaigns. In the case of Russia's influence efforts, this indirect approach often includes the use of state-owned media outlets that present their work as objective journalism, coupled with armies of both real and "bot" social media users that present themselves as Americans.

Social media has shifted the manner in which perception management campaigns work in a fundamental way: allowing foreign governments direct and personalized access to individual Americans, along with a bounty of data regarding their beliefs, interests and passions. As a result, these efforts can tailor messages to their intended audience in such a manner that they're immediately accepted as in keeping with the recipients cultural and political identity. Confirmation bias is a powerful motivator in the spread of ideas in the digital realm.

This new form of control, however, is only one facet of how perception management has become the broadest and farthest reaching form of warfare in the modern age. In nations beholden to their people such as the United States, perception is perhaps the single most significant internal factor in determining the progression and outcomes of foreign conflicts. The will of the American people fuel the drumbeat of war, bolstering recruitment numbers and stomaching casualty counts and destruction with grim determination. However, a sway of that same will in the other direction will leave politicians calling for peace in the names of their constituents. Access the will of the American people, and you gain at least some degree of control over the nation's use of its military.

The ways perception management efforts have shaped contemporary politics are already clear in some cases. Russia did work to manipulate Americans leading up to the 2016 presidential election, but America's *perception* of that act has been muddied by poor coverage and political mudslinging. Many of the American people are now more interested in victory over the opposing political party than they are in addressing the looming foreign threats on the horizon, and in no uncertain terms, that can be considered a victory for the Kremlin's ongoing efforts to tear at the fabric of American society. However, Russia is far from the only nation on earth that's working to exercise control over the narratives of our day.

China represents a far more significant threat to American military and diplomatic influence across the globe than the comparably ill-funded Russian government. However, China has long exercised its own brand of perception management -- using money in many cases to purchase influence over the American people rather than *posing* as Americans on social media. While Russia plays the role of aggressor in most international exchanges, the Chinese government ensures their nation is presented as a stable, reasonable, 21st century power.

Of course, beneath that layer of conceptual framing, Chinese propaganda efforts, both domestic and international, bely a massive espionage network set on overcoming America's military superiority, a local foreign policy of bullying and intimidation, and an advancing strategy that seeks to make China the dominant diplomatic and military power of the latter 21st Century. China sees America as an obstacle in the way of their accession into a the role of reigning superpower, and despite friendly outward appearances, they're playing for keeps.

As China, Russia and other nations use varied methodologies to engage with and manipulate the global population, the United States has fallen behind in this new form of idea warfare. Propaganda and narrative, for the most part, are seen as tools of the nefarious, and as a result, America tends to bolster falsehoods presented in bad faith by engaging with them. Russia accuses the United States of assisting ISIS in Syria, so America responds by showing proof that they aren't. In the minds of many, it's America's response, not Russia's accusation, that prompts a skeptical second thought. America, for all its power and influence, has been reluctant to engage in *planting* original narratives in the global psyche, and as a result, it has lost the advantage in the Perception Wars.

As Dr. Ajit Maan of the think tank Narrative Strategies has long argued, America's efforts need to present new narratives that discredit those of bad actors, rather than arguing with those bad actors in the public square. That isn't to say that America hasn't dabbled in some of its own perception shifting efforts over the years, however.

By Alex Hollings

The following chapters of this book are made up of stories I wrote over a two year span as a Senior Staff Writer for the military oriented news outlet, SOFREP. The stories, written as they broke, offer a glimpse into the breadth of perception management efforts over the years, starting with some historical examples that are widely unknown and culminating in the analysis of recent efforts from America and its opponents.

As long as human beings look to the horizon and wonder, as long as nations stretch further than ear shot, as long as the populous has a say in the actions of their governments, *perception* can be used as a weapon. We look out our windows to see what's going on in our neighborhoods, never once questioning the intent of the view. Then, we look to our phones, tablets, computers and televisions to see what's going on beyond our neighborhoods, and often, forget that *those views* often come with motive.

Better understanding those underlying motives, and in turn, working to inoculate ourselves against the effects of these biases, is the crux of this exploration and analysis.

Meddling with Perceptions Through History

"And if all others accepted the lie which the Party imposed—if all records told the same tale—then the lie passed into history and became truth. 'Who controls the past' ran the Party slogan, 'controls the future: who controls the present controls the past."
— George Orwell, 1984

When it comes to perception management, the old saying "fact is stranger than fiction" comes with some interesting implications. Whether it's something you believe is a *fact* or it's something you dismiss as a crackpot theory, the idea that placing that concept in front of you came as a result of a concerted information management campaign can sometimes be difficult to grasp.

The fact is, the world we live in today is heavily influenced by the perception management campaigns of previous generations. The tradition of giving a diamond ring to signify an engagement, the idea that carrots can improve your night vision, even the cultural expectation for women to shave their armpits can not only be traced back to marketing or propaganda efforts, they were born from endeavors that aren't as ancient as you might think.

In order to better understand the ways in which people work to manipulate our perceptions today, it's important that we have a thorough understanding of the successful efforts of yesterday. What follows is a collection of stories about real and alleged perception management efforts that took place in recent history... each of them comes with their own motivations, and some may be little more than an exercise in information management theory, but the implications of each remain the same: Actions are dictated by decisions, decisions are based on perceptions, and perceptions are subject to manipulation.

War may be nothing more than the continuation of politics by other means, but before a democracy goes to war, the people must believe it's the right course of action.

Was Roswell a Soviet hoax?

In July of 1947, something fell from the sky and crash landed in Mack Brazel's ranch, just northwest of Roswell, New Mexico. According to the official story, it was an experimental weather balloon. If you listen to the long list of conspiracy theories surrounding the event, it was a spaceship from another world, crewed by a species of small, large eyed, interstellar travelers; and according to investigative journalist and author Annie Jacobsen, that's just what the Soviets wanted you to think.

Annie Jacobsen isn't just another crackpot conspiracy theorist. She's a Princeton educated journalist who served as a contributing editor for The Los Angeles Times and was a finalist for the 2016 Pulitzer prize. Within the UFO community, these credentials make her stand out, but then, Jacobsen doesn't consider herself to be a member of the UFO community, even if her work has gained quite a bit of attention from within it.

In her book, "Area 51: An Uncensored History of America's Top Secret Military Base," Jacobsen posits that the infamous UFO that crashed on that fateful day in 1947 did not come from another planet, but rather from the dark recesses of Joseph Stalin's mind. Per Jacobsen's book, Stalin used Nazi technology and may have even received assistance from Josef Mengele himself, to subject the people of the United States to one of the longest standing and effective disinformation campaigns in the history of modern warfare.

Jacobsen claims to have interviewed a number of former government employees that served in various functions at the facility popular culture refers to as "Area 51" in Nevada. Area 51 has appeared in numerous movies, books and television shows as America's alien playground: where UFOs and little green men run rampant and the X-

Files is more than just a revived Fox series. The reality of the facility, of course, is a bit less exotic. Area 51, located in the dry lake bed of Groom Lake, provided the United States with a remote and secure testing facility for groundbreaking aviation advances like the U2 spy plane, the F–117 Stealth Fighter, and the A–12 Oxcart which would eventually become the SR–71 Blackbird.

The employees Jacobsen interviewed substantiated the claim that the Groom Lake air strip was used for testing new military aircraft rather than reverse engineering flying saucers. That is, until she met a engineer (who wished to remain anonymous) that claimed that he *did* spend some time dismantling and studying the wreckage of a saucer-like aircraft that was like nothing the Americans had seen before. This source, whom Jacobsen claims to "trust implicitly," relayed that the wreckage, as well as the small crew inside, were shipped to Area 51 from Wright–Patterson Air Force Base in 1951... four years after they were recovered in Roswell, New Mexico.

The crew, according to Jacobsen's book, were unfortunate casualties of a failed eugenics program, started by the Nazis and possibly even continued under Stalin after World War II. Worse still, based on their small stature, Jacobsen's source believed them to be children. Not aliens, but victims of scientific experimentation that began in the concentration camps of the Second World War.

The "spaceship" was said to be a modified Horten Ho 229 that the Soviet Union captured from the Nazi Luftwaffe during the war. Officially these (admittedly alien looking) aircraft never made it past testing, with the only one fully functioning model ever being completed before crashing during one of a handful of test flights. This aircraft was said to have been modified to accommodate three small pilots instead two full grown adults. The possibility that the craft was designed to be controlled remotely comes up in her source's description of the vehicle, as it did not seem to have any functioning control surfaces within the cabin.

The reasoning behind this elaborate craft, crew and possibly even intentional crash was supposedly to create mass hysteria within the

United States. Word of Orson Welles reading "The War of the Worlds" over the radio in 1938 causing panic among listeners had reached Josef Stalin in Moscow, and Jacobsen posits, that Stalin thought the crash of an alien spaceship could send Americans in a highly distracted frenzy. I would argue that the very concept is ridiculous, but a cursory search for the single word "Roswell" still brings about thousands of active sites postulating about alien visitors, government cover ups, and politicians being secret reptiles. If the plan was real, it may have been more effective than any of us want to give it credit for.

Of the seventy-four former Area 51 employees Jacobsen interviewed, only one said anything about a Roswell craft or its possible Soviet ties, but Jacobsen claims that the man's credentials and respectable career are the only reason she gives him claims credence. Of course, because the source chose to remain confidential, we're left to trust her judgement regarding his character.

This story, like most revolving around the infamous Roswell incident and Area 51, feels a bit too unusual to believe, but the overall quality of Jacobsen's work has earned her book attention from a number of reputable sources. Popular Mechanics, The New York Times, PBS and NPR are all among the news outlets that have interviewed Jacobsen or discussed the legitimacy of her claims, or rather the claims she relayed from former Area 51 employees.

Unlike ancient alien theorists like Giorgio Tsoukalos, who has gained prominence in recent years by suggesting that many early human advances were spurred on by extraterrestrial intervention, Jacobsen offers a new slant on the same old tales of little green men. If her book is to be believed, it would mean the true monsters are not gallivanting through the stars in search of new planets to conquer, but are actually right here on Earth. When compared to the likelihood that an advanced alien civilization was able to successfully navigate the galaxy only to go down in flames over the American Southwest, her claims begin to feel a bit less ludicrous.

As unlikely as alien-looking test subjects being flown remotely from the Soviet Union to trick the American public may seem, this may be the only scenario where such a story could be considered the more likely hypothesis. For this writer's money, though, a fallen weather balloon still seems like the most likely culprit.

The White House memo to be used if Apollo 11's crew became stranded on the moon

On July 21st, 1969, human history changed forever. With a single step, Neil Armstrong became the first human in history to reach another world; a feat man had dreamed of accomplishing since time immemorial.

Only eight years prior, President John F. Kennedy assumed the responsibility of convincing Congress that sending a manned mission to the moon was not only possible, but it was necessary in order to catch up to and overtake the Soviet Union, who had, until that point, been the leader in space fairing endeavors for all of humanity. Kennedy knew that only by placing an American flag on the closest celestial body to our own planet could America hope to declare victory in the space race, which would have far-reaching ramifications in another sort of race the U.S. and Soviet Union were competing in: the arms race of the Cold War.

In many ways, the early American space program was a war-time effort, and the men and women involved in the Gemini and Apollo missions were aware of that. While modern NASA places the safety of its astronauts above all else, the first men to leave Earth's embrace with an American flag sewn on their arm were offered no such reassurances. In fact, early Gemini capsules didn't contain any kind of controls... the human occupants were merely along for the ride and served primarily as lab rats, simply to see if the trip was even survivable.

By Alex Hollings

In the days leading up to Apollo 11's launch, that same mindset permeated not only those tasked with preparing for and executing the launch, but in all facets of the American government. Indeed, the astronauts involved with the Apollo program were not even able to secure life insurance policies before climbing atop the modified intercontinental ballistic missile intended to take them into space, leaving them with no alternative but to sign autographs on 8×10 photos for their wives to sell if the worst were to occur. These men knew, each time they strapped themselves to a rocket, that there was a distinct possibility that they would never set foot on their home planet again, and they accepted that risk in earnest, because they believed the ultimate goal of putting an American on the moon was bigger than any individual life. Like so many American heroes before them and since, the astronauts of the Gemini and Apollo missions valued the success and progress of their nation over their own wellbeing.

Because everyone involved understood and appreciated the risks in shooting men at the moon only 66 years after the Wright brothers first took flight, the government had to prepare for the possibility that Neil Armstrong and Buzz Aldrin may never make the trip back home once they reached their destination. Any number of complications could cause them to die before ever reaching the moon's surface, and conducting a second successful launch from that surface and back to the orbiter more than doubled the chances for failure.

Eight years prior, President Kennedy had convinced Congress to fund the greatest expedition in human history, but on July 21st of 1969, President Nixon faced the possibility of having to tell the American people that their heroes were never coming home.

Bill Safire, a columnist for the New York Times and speechwriter for President Nixon, was assigned the unenviable task of writing remarks for the President to deliver to the American people in the event Neil Armstrong and Buzz Aldrin found themselves stranded on the moon's surface. With the technological capabilities available to NASA, the government knew any issue with the lander's launch ability was a death sentence, as there was no hope of sending a rescue mission.

In a short two-page memo shown in its entirely below and housed in the presidential archives, Safire encompassed the gratitude the American people felt for these brave men risking their lives on behalf of their country and their world, and gave us a glimpse into the fears running through the minds of the American people in those fateful days leading up to one of America's greatest heroes taking that "giant leap for mankind."

Read the speech and directions for clergyman below:

To H. R. Haldeman
From: Bill Safire   July 18, 1969.

IN EVENT OF MOON DISASTER:

Fate has ordained that the men who went to the moon to explore in peace will stay on the moon to rest in peace.

These brave men, Neil Armstrong and Edwin Aldrin, know that there is no hope for their recovery. But they also know that there is hope for mankind in their sacrifice.

These two men are laying down their lives in mankind's most noble goal: the search for truth and understanding.

They will be mourned by their families and friends; they will be mourned by their nation; they will be mourned by the people of the world; they will be mourned by a Mother Earth that dared send two of her sons into the unknown.

In their exploration, they stirred the people of the world to feel as one; in their sacrifice, they bind more tightly the brotherhood of man.

In ancient days, men looked at stars and saw their heroes in the constellations. In modern times, we do much the same, but our heroes are epic men of flesh and blood.

Others will follow, and surely find their way home. Man's search will not be denied. But these men were the first, and they will remain the foremost in our hearts.

For every human being who looks up at the moon in the nights to come will know that there is some corner of another world that is forever mankind.

PRIOR TO THE PRESIDENT'S STATEMENT:
The President should telephone each of the widows -to-be.
AFTER THE PRESIDENT'S STATEMENT, AT THE POINT WHEN NASA ENDS COMMUNICATIONS WITH THE MEN:
A clergyman should adopt the same procedure as a burial at sea, commending their souls to "the deepest of the deep," concluding with the Lord's Prayer.

Did the U.S. really spend millions on a space pen while the Soviets just used pencils?

We've all heard the story. Back in the 1960s, as the Americans and Soviets were competing for space (and global) supremacy, the United States supposedly spent millions to develop a pen that their astronauts could use in space. The Soviets, meanwhile, "just used a pencil." It's a classic tale used to criticize government spending and incompetent bureaucracy, and is even used to take a jab at the victors of the Space Race—NASA and the American people. But just how true is this story?

After all, I've previously written about the near "blank check" methodology used by the government to fund the F-35 Joint Strike Fighter, and that's far from the silliest expenditure one can come up with regarding government spending. In 2015, a government grant provided $1.3 million to two University of Washington students to study how a koozie keeps your drink cold on a hot day.[1] It seems totally possible that, while the scrappy Soviet Union had the wherewithal to use pencils in space, we here under the red, white, and blue decided to toss funds away on another unnecessary program.

But truth is always more complicated than parable.

In the early days of manned space travel, both Americans and Soviets used pencils to fill out paperwork and take notes while in orbit.[2] Pencils, however, weren't very good to use in the micro-gravity environment of low-Earth orbit. While pencils are erasable (always handy) and don't contain any liquid that could feasibly leak out into the space capsule, they were plagued by other issues. Wooden shavings proved to be a real problem, as they could float freely inside the capsule and gunk up equipment, get caught in an astronaut's eye, or get breathed in and irritate an astronaut's throat. Mechanical pencils were only slightly better, leaving flecks of graphite floating around in the capsule as they were used. It's worth noting, as well, that space capsules are an oxygen-rich environment, which makes the use of anything flammable, like a wooden pencil, a risky endeavor.

Regular pens couldn't work in orbit because they were designed down here on Earth where gravity provides a consistent force to drive the ink out of the pen and onto the page. Pens don't work upside down for the same reason they won't work in orbit: The ink simply stays put in the body of the pen without a force pushing it outward.

Enter Paul C. Fisher.[3] Fisher wasn't an astronaut, nor was he a government scientist or bureaucrat. Fisher owned the Fisher Pen Company, which invested over a million dollars into the development of a pen that would work regardless of gravity's presence. Neither NASA, nor the government at large, provided any of the seed funding. Fisher had designed the pen to be used in all kinds of hazardous environments, including extreme cold or heat, but he hadn't initially had space in mind. He simply wanted to create something people could use if their work prevented them from writing in the traditional, pen-pointed-down method.

NASA was hesitant initially, but after extensive testing, they opted to adopt the Fisher Space Pen as their primary writing utensil for all further missions. They placed a bulk order and paid a price of $2.39 per pen.

The pen used a replaceable pressurized ink cartridge to force the ink out of the tip regardless of gravitational pull, and testing showed that these pens proved extremely reliable in all sorts of circumstances and conditions. The ink was kept from pouring out of the pen by adding a small amount of resin to change its viscosity. The pens proved so effective, in fact, the Soviet Union also placed a bulk order with the Fisher Pen Company for his patented space pens, paying the exact same price per pen as their U.S competition -- contrary to the stories about NASA's rampant spending that were so often touted by Soviet media outlets.

So, while the old story may paint the Soviet Union as the savvier party in the Space Race, the truth of the matter was, good old fashioned American capitalism not only won the race, it also gave the cosmonauts the pens they used to write their reports about it.

Maybe that means we could still be in store for a koozie breakthrough, too.

By Alex Hollings

Soviet secrets: Are there dead cosmonauts in orbit above Earth?

On April 12th, 1961, a Russian man named Yuri Gagarin made history aboard a Soviet Vostok 3KA-3 spacecraft. For years, the United States and Soviet Union had been using the barrier between our world and beyond as a benchmark to test each nation's greatest technological and engineering advances, and on that day, Gagarin achieved an incredible victory for the communist nation: he flew in space.

The space race was about far more than national pride, however, it was truly about global supremacy. Each nation recognized the final frontier as both a tactical advantage for military operations and a public relations necessity – competition put the American people behind spending the money required to go up against the Red giant, and victory would benefit morale nationwide. However, the Soviets did not need the public's approval for expenditures, opting instead to announce each mission toward the unknown only after its successful completion, leaving their people under the impression that the Soviet program was *incapable of failure.*

In recent years, however, stories have begun to emerge about failed Soviet space missions and their policy of ensuring the media, the public, and their American competition never learned of their missteps.

Photographs surfaced in the 1970s depicting early Cosmonauts (Soviet Astronauts) at work and on vacation with one another, but because of confusion regarding which photographs had been published, Soviet news managers accidentally released never before seen versions of the images. When previously published images were compared to the images that were released in the seventies, inconsistencies began caught the public's attention. Most notable among these issues were missing Cosmonauts; the Soviet government had actually airbrushed entire people out of group photographs, opting to pretend these men were never a part of the program to begin with.

When confronted about these alterations, the Soviet Government made a number of fumbled attempts at explaining why they felt the need to forge the images released to the public. Finally, in the final years of Soviet reign, Gorbachev instructed Soviet journalists and historians to determine what truly happened to these "missing" and omitted men. Their research revealed that most had been expelled from the program for behavior that made them unsuitable to be seen as heroes for the nation, or had developed medical conditions that prohibited them from participating in space flight. According to reports, the Soviet government had opted to remove them from records completely rather than explain away their failures in public.

All of this did little to sway American beliefs that the Soviets, even years after America claimed victory in the space race by landing on the moon, had more to hide than they were letting on. While some Americans have gone so far as to travel to Russia to meet with some of these redacted cosmonauts to verify Soviet stories, not all of the men can be accounted for officially.

American author and former NASA mission control scientist, James Oberg, was one of the first to notice the inconsistencies in the Soviet images and, although he has written at length about his beliefs regarding these "lost" cosmonauts in books like "Uncovering Soviet Disasters," he seems fairly convinced in recent years that the Soviets were telling the truth about these redactions, and that most, if not all, of these missing cosmonauts were simply removed from the space program photographs to protect their flawless reputation.[4]

Possibly the most damning, or at least the most controversial, evidence to suggest that the Soviet space program was not nearly as flawless as they contended at the time, were reports of a pair of Italian brothers that recorded radio transmissions prior to and after Gagarin's historic flight that seemed to indicate manned orbital missions going awry.[5]

The Judica-Cordiglia brothers were amateur ham radio operators that released a number of recordings in 1963 that they claimed were made during the Soviet's most intense period of attempts to put a cosmonaut in space; attempts which they claim began in 1960, nearly a year prior to Gagarin's successful mission.

According to the brothers, in May of 1960 they recorded a Morse code message indicating that a manned Soviet spacecraft had drifted dangerously off course. Then, on November 28th, 1960, another Morse code signal, this time an SOS distress call, was recorded as another spacecraft reportedly left Earth's orbit. In February of 1961, they recorded a cosmonaut audibly suffocating to death while attempting to contact mission control, then in April, they tracked Gagarin's vessel as it made three successful orbits around Earth before reentering. The Soviets announced Gagarin's success three days after the brothers claim to have tracked his flight path.

The recordings did not stop there, however. In May, the brothers claimed to have recorded another craft's distress call as it slipped out of orbit, then again in October and November. In November of 1963, the brothers said they recorded a female cosmonaut pleading for help as her craft burned up during reentry.[6] A final death, according to these brothers, occurred in April of 1964, again due to failed heat shielding during the return flight.

There are confirmed reports of Soviets dying in their pursuit of space flight, but these reports were often not confirmed until after the fall of the Soviet Union and in the face of overwhelming evidence. Gagarin's own best friend died in an orbital mission.[7] According to claims, he was aware that his mission was likely to fail due to a number of structural issues on the vessel, but opted to fly anyway to prevent his friend and backup pilot, the Soviet hero Gagarin, from having to take the risk. While it is confirmed that Vladimir Kamarov died during the failed re-entry of his Soyuz 1 capsule, rumors continue to surface about his final minutes, in which many claim he railed against the Soviet regime and faulted them for his impending death.

Twenty-two Americans have died as a result of our own efforts to extend mankind's reach beyond our tiny blue dot.[8] The task is incredibly dangerous and the men and women of every nation's space program should be heralded for their bravery, but if claims about Soviet efforts to erase the lives of men and women that were lost in pursuit of victory over America are even partially true, it would add a dark lens to how we perceive all Soviet accomplishments during the era.

By Alex Hollings

The Nazino Affair: Russia's Cannibal Island

Russia is a vast nation, with huge expanses of undeveloped land in parts of the country that are generally considered to be difficult or impossible to cultivate. Soviet leaders were not unaware of the possible untapped potential this uninhabited land presented, so in 1933, Genrikh Yagoda, the head of the Russian secret police, and Matvei Berman, head of the Gulag or Soviet labor camp system, devised a plan to establish settlements throughout Siberia and Kazakhstan.

The Soviet Union began with the forced relocation of kulaks, which was a class of farming peasants that lost favor with the Soviet regime for failing to hand over their harvests to local government officials.[9] These farmers met extremely limited success on the lands they were forced to occupy, due in large part to drought and their methods of sharecropping. The limitations, however, did not dissuade the Soviet regime from continuing to expel those they deemed unworthy of inclusion in proper Soviet society.

In the Spring of 1933, Soviet troops, under the direction of Yagoda and Berman, began rounding up "socially harmful elements" in Moscow and Leningrad.[10] Some of these citizens were petty criminals, but most were merchants or traders. Some were chosen simply because they did not appear to fit the idealized image of a communist citizen. Arrests were primarily justified by claiming the citizens failed to acquire or present domestic travel passports, even when arrested within the communities they resided in. Deportees were processed and transported within two days of their arrest, not allowed to communicate with anyone, and could give their loved ones no notice of their expulsion.

Between March and July of 1933, it was reported that more than 90,000 Soviet citizens were deported to other locations in the Soviet Union from the Moscow and Leningrad areas. The vast majority of these deportees were transferred from the Tomsk transit camp to farms elsewhere, but more than 6,000 that were given the label "outdated elements" were sent instead to Nazino Island, a small and isolated patch of land in Western Siberia where the Ob and Nazina Rivers meet.

Among that six thousand people were nearly two thousand criminals, sent to the island in an effort to "decongest" the Soviet prison system. The majority of the remainder were "urban outdated elements" – people expelled from major cities and transported with no food, tools or supplies. Their trip was divided into two legs; the first was by train, where each deportee was given a daily ration of three hundred grams of bread. The second leg was by barges designed to ship wood, where each deportee's ration was cut down to two hundred grams of bread.

Crime among the deportees began almost immediately, as hunger pushed them toward desperation. The barges carried twenty tons of flour (enough to give each deportee almost nine pounds), as well as fifty or so newly recruited guards.

Nazino island, a three kilometer long, six hundred meter wide, swampy patch of earth amid two powerful rivers offered no shelter, farmable land, or sufficient tree growth to harvest firewood. When the barges arrived, twenty-seven deportees had already succumbed to the hunger and poor conditions. The remaining people were unloaded onto the island, provided their rations of flour, and left with no other tools, equipment or supplies. The following day, about twelve hundred additional deportees were delivered to the island with no additional rations or equipment.

Because they had no means to cook the flour they had, many simply mixed it with the river water in order to eat it, leading to widespread infections that led to dysentery for many. Criminal elements immediately began establishing territories and confiscating rations from those too weak to stop them. Some attempted to build rafts in order to make their escape, but because the powerful current could only take the rafts back to Tomsk, most accepted their fate and chose to remain. Those who attempted to leave were hunted by guards on patrol. Accounts from Nazino survivors tell of the bodies of hopeful escapees washing back up on the shores of the island by the hundreds. Two hundred and ninety-five people died on the first day alone.

By May 21st, only eleven days after the majority of the deportees arrived on the island, three health officers observed five confirmed cases of cannibalism between the island's new forced residents. Although there were no other available sources of food on the island, the guards immediately banned the practice and began arresting those they observed killing and eating one another. Within the next thirty days, they arrested fifty more people for cannibalism.

One survivor account explained that while many of the guards killed the island inhabitants without hesitation, some did establish bonds with the starving people.[11] One guard was reported to have even been courting a young woman on the island. When he was called away, he asked a friend to watch over her, but the friend proved unable.

"People caught the girl, tied her to a poplar tree, cut off her breasts, her muscles, everything they could eat, everything, everything.... They were hungry, they had to eat. When Kostia came back, she was still alive. He tried to save her, but she had lost too much blood."

Unbeknownst to those left on the island, Stalin was presented with the updated plan at nearly the same time they were beginning to arrive. He rejected it out of hand, but the gears of Soviet Russia were slow to turn, and fate of thousands had already been sealed.

By June, only 3,013 of the estimated 6,700 island inhabitants were still alive. The majority of the survivors were relocated to smaller, better supplied settlements, but 157 proved too weak to leave the island at all, with many more dying en route to their new camps. Once there, many more succumbed to typhus infection. By October, Soviet records indicate less than three hundred were still capable of any kind of work.

In 1988, the President of the Soviet Union, Mikhail Gorbachev, began a government transparency program commonly referred to as Glasnost. Through this program, records of what occurred on Nazino Island were finally released to the public, proving that the events that had prompted folk songs and legends throughout the nation had actually occurred. Although the records included the number of people brought to the islands, as well as the number confirmed dead, the names of the deportees were never recorded, leaving the families of those who died forever unsure as to the fate of their loved ones.

The Russian Memorial Society as well as local organizations surrounding Nazino Island have since erected a cross on the site of this tragic chapter in Soviet history. The simple stone monument reads only, "For the innocent victims of the years of unbelief." In 2012, during a ceremony, the Memorial Society read off the names of those few who could be confirmed to have died on the island, but the identities of most may never be known.

Author's Note

Following the release of this story, a number of people, many of whom appeared to be Russian citizens, accused me of falsifying the accounts of this story. While my sources with cited throughout and the Russian government does not deny what happened on Nazino Island, the disinformation effort tied to this dark part of Russia's history remains effective to this day.

By Alex Hollings

Conspiracy theories the KGB planted in the US that you might still believe

Every national government, like every major corporation, has to make a concerted effort to control perceptions—both internally and externally. For a government, internal communications are often ripe with propaganda. Whether it's encouraging you to support a war effort, steering you toward a specific political party, or trying to convince you that the people in power have your best interests at heart, an integral part of domestic communications is swaying the populace toward the policies of the powerful. It's not as evil as it sounds—it's literally the basis of our political system.

OK, so maybe it is as evil as it sounds, then.

But what about external communications? How do you sway a populace in another country — one that's already subjected to the propaganda of its own complex political infrastructure — to see things your way? Even more difficult, how do you manage the perceptions of people that live in a nation that sees *you* as the enemy? Russia has found itself facing these very questions time and time again when it comes to controlling American opinions. That's right, Russia didn't just start attempting to manipulate Americans in the 2016 election. International disinformation campaigns are as historically Russian as apple pie is American—and they've been successful to boot.

What was Russia's answer to those difficult questions? Easy. Convince the American people that *their own government* is the real bad guy.

The JFK assassination

Everyone has heard a conspiracy theory tied to the assassination of President John F. Kennedy. For those who were alive at the time, the day JFK was shot would be permanently branded into their consciousness by tragedy, but it didn't take long for some people to start worrying about how the details of the case added up, and to start looking for alternate, more malicious theories to explain the horrible events that took place in Dallas that fateful day. Soon, people began tossing about ideas involving any number of America's three-letter agencies, accusing the CIA or FBI, in particular, of having something to do with the death of the president.

Theories involving Soviet involvement are somehow less popular, despite the fact that his killer, Lee Harvey Oswald, taught himself the Russian language and spent time within the communist state.[12] The Soviets were America's biggest boogeymen at the time, so it seems a bit odd that people would look first to the agencies tasked with protecting our nation when grasping for a malicious secret, rather than the country that prompted school kids to practice hiding under their desks in case of a world-ending nuclear attack...but it turns out there's a pretty good reason for that.

In 1992, Vasili Mitrokhin, a KGB archivist who served in the foreign intelligence service for more than 30 years, defected to the U.K., and he brought the Mitrokhin Archive with him. This archive of handwritten notes contained documents that laid out a number of the Soviet Union's clandestine intelligence operations from all over the globe. Christopher Andrew, MI5's official historian, would use the information contained in the archive to write two books, "Sword and the Shield" (1999) and "The KGB and the Battle for the Third World" (2005).

The information contained within the archive was bounced against what British and American intelligence agencies were able to confirm, prompting the FBI, the U.S. Air Force, the American Historical Review, and the British Parliament to confirm the archive's authenticity.

One of the most interesting portions of the archive contained the elaborate plot to spread disinformation about Kennedy's death within the United States. Now, that isn't to say that the Soviets invented all of the conspiracy theories people continue to cling to today. As the archive points out, the Soviets were spurred on by America's ability to produce their own craziness. The Soviets just worked to encourage it.

The Soviets even went so far as to use samples of Oswald's writing to produce a forged letter from him to a known CIA operative, discussing a secret meeting they would both attend days before the assassination.[13] The forgery was so good, even Oswald's wife confirmed it to be his handwriting. The New York Times had three writing experts confirm its authenticity, adding credibility to every tinfoil hat-wearing homeless guy's belief that it was the CIA, not a lone gunman, that killed their beloved president.

The real JFK conspiracy was how the Soviets capitalized on the tragedy to sow seeds of doubt between the American people and their government — seeds that continue to germinate in the form of 9/11 "truthers" to this day.

HIV/AIDS as a weapon

Growing up in the '80s and '90s, my fears weren't really tied to nuclear annihilation the way they may have been for the older generation at the time. Instead, popular culture taught me to be terrified of a different kind of death: AIDS.

Even as a kid, I heard rumors about where HIV came from. Some kids said it came from someone having sex with a monkey, but the weirder kids that chimed in had an equally crazy assessment, one that would gradually take hold in the minds of many Americans: The government invented it to reduce homosexual and African American populations.

In 2005, the Rand Corporation conducted a poll in which they asked around 500 African Americans what they thought about HIV and AIDS. Just about half admitted to believing it was a man-made weapon created in U.S. government laboratories, with around 12 percent citing the CIA specifically.[14] Another study conducted that same year by the National Institute of Child Health and Human Development found a similar result. Fifteen percent even went so far as to say that they believed AIDS was a form of government-sponsored genocide targeting the African-American community.

Although the United States has plenty to be ashamed of in the way it has treated African Americans throughout its history, it still seems like a stretch to assume that the government was targeting American citizens with a biological weapon. So where did this concept come from?

You guessed it. In 1992, former Russian Intelligence Chief and Prime Minister Yevgeni Primakov admitted openly that the Soviet Union had worked to plant that idea in the minds of Americans. They had dubbed the covert disinformation campaign "Operation Infektion," because a bad joke isn't lost on the kinds of folks that do this sort of work.

They began by planting stories in international news outlets about HIV/AIDS outbreaks occurring in a number of nations, connecting those outbreaks to fictional U.S. biological weapons tests.[15] They used media outlets that they secretly controlled (not unlike they do today with sites like Sputnik and RT) to then publish additional stories about HIV, citing the previous stories about American biological weapons within the articles published by seemingly unrelated news organizations. The Soviets even went so far as to include messages about the American government creating AIDS in pornography intended for Western distribution, because anything worth doing is worth doing in all of the craziest ways you can imagine. One prominent German biophysicist even published a paper about America "engineering" AIDS as a result of the Soviets efforts.

But the craziest thing about the story is that it worked.

By Alex Hollings

Rasputin's death may have saved the allies in WWI: Here's how it really happened

The legend of Grigori Rasputin, commonly referred to as simply, "Rasputin," has a significant reach. Even before I was aware of the tsarist government in Russia that allowed his rise to power, before I know who Tsar Nicholas II was, pop-culture had left me acutely aware of the Russian mystic that proved so difficult to kill, his death became the stuff of legend. Like Aleister Crowley, those heavily involved with the occult look to men like Rasputin as undeniable proof of the power available to human beings if they could only master a twisted and darkly real version of Harry Potter's spells.

Little is known about the early life of Rasputin, though there's plenty of conjecture. What we can surmise for sure is that he was likely born in January of 1869, and by 1897 he had converted and joined the Russian Orthodox Church. Despite holding no official position within the church, he managed to captivate church and social leaders while on a pilgrimage sometime between 1903 and 1905, and by November of 1905, he met the man who would be the final Tsar of Russia, Tsar Nicholas II.

Nicholas II had only one heir to inherit the throne, but the child's hemophilia threatened to leave the Russian nation without a dynastic replacement for its leader. Enter the mystic healer Rasputin, who captivated both the Tsar and his wife, Alexandra.

Soon, Rasputin had developed a powerful rapport with the Russian Tsar, and with many others in the nation. Russians far and wide saw him as a powerful mystic, a magician, and even a prophet. Still, many others within the Russian elite saw him as something else entirely: a charlatan, and more importantly, a threat.

The story of Rasputin's death was relayed by the powerful Russians that claimed to have killed him, and seemingly eager to demonstrate their own power, they painted a picture that was in keeping with Rasputin's reputation. A group of Russian nobles, led by Prince Felix Yusupov, the Grand Duke Dmitri Pavlovich, and the politician Vladimir Purishkevich lured the mystic to Yusupov's Moika Palace with an invitation from Moika's wife. According to their tale, they led the man to the cellar, where they fed him cakes and red wine laced with what should have been more than enough cyanide to kill "five men;" yet he remained unaffected.

Prince Yusupov grew concerned that the poison may be taking too long to take effect, allowing the man to survive the night and potentially to reveal their crime, so he spoke to his co-conspirators before coming back downstairs and shooting Rasputin in the back with a revolver. After the shooting, the group chose to leave the palace for a bit, but Yusupov claimed that he returned to the basement for his jacket – only to have Rasputin's body regain consciousness and lunge at him in an attempt to strangle his killer. The other conspirators, apparently nearby, leapt into action, firing three more shots into his back. Rasputin fell to the floor, and as they approached him to confirm he was finally dead, they were shocked to find him awake and struggling to get back to his feet. They clubbed him repeatedly until he stopped moving, and according to some legends, they severed his penis for good measure, before binding him and wrapping him in a carpet like the victim in a poorly written movie.

The group of conspirators then, per their own accounts, tossed Rasputin's body into the icy Neva River. When his body was recovered days later, doctors claimed to find more than enough poison to kill a man in his system – but more interestingly – water in his lungs, suggesting that the Russian magician had survived the poison, shootings, beatings, and possible even the penis-severing, only to finally succumb to drowning when he couldn't escape his carpeted prison.

Of course, the story was corroborated by those involved, eager to secure their own places in Russian history amidst a revolution that would end the Romanov Dynasty and the rule of Rasputin's benefactor, Tsar Nicholas II... but can we really believe this account of events? Could Rasputin truly have been immune to poison, maybe even to gun shots and blunt force trauma? Could he *really* have possessed some kind of other-worldly power?

Chances are... no. In fact, Rasputin's death likely played out more like the end scene of a Bond movie, rather than something written by J.K Rowling.[16]

"I am 99.9 percent certain of this," claims Richard Cullen, a retired Scotland Yard commander who studied the case alongside Andrew Cook, an intelligence historian.

"There is a fair weight of evidence to show that Rayner was the man. We have conclusive proof that the previously accepted versions of events are fabrications."[17]

See, although Rasputin's magical abilities are subject to doubt, his ability to manipulate people certainly wasn't. A religious "pilgrim" that somehow managed to secure a seat as the Russian Tsar's most trusted advisor didn't get there with card tricks, after all, and there is a fair amount of evidence to suggest that Rasputin was brokering a deal on behalf of the Tsar with Germany – and it being 1916 meant such a deal could be disastrous for the Allied powers in the first World War. Peace between Russia and Germany would free up hundreds of thousands of troops, and make the Western front of the war effort dramatically more difficult to win.

Oswald Rayner was a member of Britain's Secret Intelligence Bureau and was working at the Russian court in St Petersburg, not far from the location of Rasputin's murder. Forensic analysis of Rasputin's body, and of images taken at the scene seem to contradict the legend, showing only three bullet holes in the magician's body – each from different caliber firearms; one of which, was fired at close range, and directly to the forehead.

As it would turn out, Prince Yusupov, who did have real motive to kill the advisor to the Tsar, was also close friends with Rayner thanks to studying together in college years prior. According to Cullen, that third and final shot that killed Rasputin actually came from the British spy's gun.

By piecing together the evidence, Cullen and Cook were able to surmise that Rasputin was indeed shot in the back by Yusupov and his co-conspirator Purishkevich (accounting for the first two, different caliber, bullet holes in his body). As they carried Rasputin's body across the courtyard to the car, Rasputin likely began to twitch, which was when Rayner promptly dispatched the last remnants of life from the unconscious man via close range shot to the head.[18]

Rayner's cover was maintained by the British government, and on the Russian side by the conspirators that helped conduct the assassination, as their involvement made them heroes within the revolution. This account of the events that took place that fateful night is supported by a memo on file that was sent between Rayner's two superiors in St. Petersburg, John Scale and Stephen Alley, which read:

"Although matters have not proceeded entirely to plan, our objective has clearly been achieved. Reaction to the demise of 'Dark Forces' [a codename for Rasputin] has been well received by all, although a few awkward questions have already been asked about wider involvement. Rayner is attending to loose ends and will no doubt brief you on your return."

If Rayner truly was responsible for the bullet that killed the very-mortal Rasputin, he never fessed up. After leaving Russia prior to the end of the war, he took a job at The Daily Telegraph and served quietly as a Finnish correspondent until retiring to Botley, Oxfordshire to serve as a fund-raiser for his church until his death in 1965. He was survived by one son, John Felix Rayner. By Rayner's own accounts, his son's middle name, "Felix," was in honor of Rayner's good friend, Prince

Felix Yusupov – whom history credits with the Russian wizard's demise.

Rasputin's final trick, however, has managed to take hold in the minds of many... as he continues to be revered by occultists around the world, and there's something to be said for that.

Cold War comedy: Read the CIA's classified list of official jokes about the Soviet Union

The CIA webpage is an oft under-appreciated gem in the U.S. government's suite of dry, formal websites. There's no formal decree that mandates government sites have to be boring, but something about the need to exude inoffensive professionalism throughout every corner of these sprawling domains has sanitized everything .GOV into the digital version of the Department of Motor Vehicles, including, of course, the websites devoted to the various DMVs throughout the nation.

Despite their similarities in presentation, government websites are not uniform in content or even their organization. If you know your way around the Pentagon's website (Defense.gov), you can rest assured that the State Department's (State.gov) won't operate in an even remotely similar way, meaning digging for the information you're on the market for requires a different method at each of Uncle Sam's sites. If you're on the hunt for a specific thing, this can be frustrating, as you bounce between government sites trying to assemble a complete picture of American policy in action, rather than in *description*, like you tend to get from press releases. But if you're *not* digging for something in particular, you'd be surprised at some of the things you can find, as long as you're willing to suffer the frustrations of digital bureaucracy in motion.

Which brings us to the *hands down* winner of most fun way to spend your Sunday night on a .GOV website: CIA.GOV. When their site first loads, you're greeted (currently) by a lovely story about a puppy that wasn't cut out for life as a service dog in the CIA, for instance. It's as if to say, "sure, you've heard about our covert operations all over the world, but why don't you check out this puppy instead of whatever you came here for?"

Okay, CIA. You guys are good.

When you reach that homepage, you're only a few clicks away from a goldmine: the CIA's Freedom of Information Archive. This archive is comprised of all kinds of fun documents that have been declassified through the efforts of previous internet explorers (and likely, a good number that stuck to paper) – including all kinds of UFO and alien related content, studies about psychic powers and ESP, and of course, lots and lots of Cold War era Soviet analysis.

You may be thinking, "Soviet analysis? That's not very much fun..." – but you'd be wrong. It's easy to look back on our country's simmering fight against the Soviet Union as a collection of Reagan quotes and square jawed generals looking to the horizon with gritted teeth, but just like today, America recognized the need to appear socially and culturally relevant in its efforts. Your average American was just as prone to escapism and the need for a good joke to cut the tension as modern Americans are. Perhaps, it's because of that that this list was put together: which is titled simply, "SOVIET JOKES FOR THE DDCI."

The Deputy Director of Central Intelligence (DDCI) undoubtedly had to attend a number of social events, in which he needed to schmooze with other high ranking officials or prominent civilian figures, and he needed to be able to keep the effort *cool* by cracking jokes about America's number one enemy. Or maybe these jokes were intended for public addresses, so he could demonstrate his confidence in the face of the Soviet threat. Maybe he just loved a good cheesy joke. In any regard, it's fun to read through them with the understanding that this was our federal government's honest attempt at equipping its senior leadership with the *latest* in anti-Soviet verbal weaponry.

The fact that these jokes were kept classified might indicate that they weren't intended for wide distribution, or maybe, just that the

Deputy Director didn't want the world to know he wasn't that witty on his own...

By Alex Hollings

DDCI

Soviet Jokes for the DDCI

A worker standing in a liquor line says, "I have had enough, save my place, I am going to shoot Gorbachev." Two hours later he returns to claim his place in line. His friends ask, "Did you get him?" No, the line there was even longer than the line here."

"What's the difference between Gorbachev and Dubcek?" Nothing, but Gorbachev doesn't know it yet.

Sentence from a schoolboy's weekly composition class essay - "My cat just had seven kittens. They are all communists." Sentence from same boy's composition the following week - "My cat's seven kittens are all capitalists." Teacher reminds boy that the previous week he had said the kittens were communists. "But now they've opened their eyes," replies the child.

A Chukchi is asked what he would do if the Soviet borders were opened. "I'd climb the highest tree," he replies. Asked why, he responds: "So I wouldn't get trampled in the stampede out!" Then he is asked what he would do if the U.S. border is opened. "I'd climb the highest tree," he says, "So I can see the first person crazy enough to come here!"

A joke heard in Arkhangelsk has it that someone happened to call the KGB headquarters just after a major fire. "We cannot do anything. The KGB has just burned down" he was told. Five minutes later he called back and was told again that the KGB had burned. When he called a third time, the telephone operator recognized his voice and asked, "Why do you keep calling back? I just told you, the KGB has burned down." "I know," the man replied. "I just like to hear it."

A train bearing Lenin, Stalin, Khrushchev, Brezhnev and Gorbachev stops suddenly when the tracks run out. Each leader applies his own, unique solution. Lenin gathers workers and peasants from miles around and exhorts them to build more track. Stalin shoots the train crew when the train still doesn't move. Khrushchev rehabilitates the dead crew and orders the tracks behind the train ripped up and relaid in front. Brezhnev pulls down the curtains and rocks back and forth, pretending the train is moving. And Gorbachev calls a rally in front of the locomotive, where he leads a chant: "No tracks! No tracks! No tracks!"

Ivanov: Give me a medical example of perstroyka.
Sidorov: (Thinks) How about menopause?

An old lady goes to the Gorispolkom with a question, but by the time she
gets to the official's office she has forgotten the purpose of the visit.
"Was it about your pension?" the official asks. "No, I get 20 rubles a
month, that's fine," she replies. "About your apartment?" "No, I live
with three people in one room of a communal apartment, I'm fine," she
replies. Suddenly she remembers: "Who invented communism--the communists
or scientists?" The official responds proudly, "Why the communists, of
course!" "That's what I thought," the babushka says. "If the scientists
had invented it, they would have tested it first on dogs!"

An American tells a Russian that the United States is so free he can stand
in front of the White House and yell, "To hell with Ronald Reagan." The
Russian replies: "That's nothing. I can stand in front of the Kremlin and
yell, 'To hell with Ronald Reagan,' too."

A man goes into a shop and asks "You don't have any meat?" "No, replies
the sales lady, "We don't have any fish. It's the store across the street
that doesn't have any meat."

A man is driving with his wife and small child. A militia man pulls them
over and makes the man take a breathalyzer test. "See," the militia man
says, "you're drunk." The man protests that the breathalyzer must be
broken and invites the cop to test his wife. She also registers as drunk.
Exasperated, the man invites the cop to test his child. When the child
registers drunk as well, the cop shrugs, says, "Yes, perhaps it is broken,"
and send them on their way. Out of earshot the man tells his wife, "See, I
told you it wouldn't hurt to give the kid five grams of vodka."

By Alex Hollings

World War II, Nazi bombers and... carrots? How propaganda even shapes what we eat

In many ways, the modern media landscape goes out of its way to ensure your average person doesn't *really* know for sure what type of diet is good for them. Diet fads are a multi-billion-dollar a year industry, and they invest quite a bit of money into keeping the "secret" to shedding excess weight seem like some proprietary breakthrough. They fund massive campaigns intended to sell you on the idea that, in order to be healthy, you need to exorcise the fat demons from your body by only eating like a caveman, a baby deer or a turn of the century farmer.

Even the debate between conventional produce versus organic is continually muddied by biased studies funded by lobbies on either side. For instance, the data doesn't really support the idea that a strictly organic diet is healthier, but variables like pesticide use and misleading studies make it difficult to know which elements of which diet are *actually* better for you, and which are just a part of a concerted marketing campaign aimed at selling you an eight dollar jar of water with a bit of asparagus in it.[19] The thing is, confusion about what effect different types of food have on your body is nothing new, and you may even still believe some dietary myths that were born out of marketing or even *propaganda* campaigns that were prevalent in your parent's or grandparent's youth.

SOFREP readers are, by and large, rather savvy when it comes to all sorts of things, healthy living included. Still, even smart, experienced and educated people are susceptible to being misled by pervasive misconceptions, especially when they're delivered by government officials and have a loose basis in scientific fact. One such program gained quite a bit of notoriety just a few years ago, when Domino's Pizza found its sales lagging behind the competition and realized that it might be because their pizza didn't actually *taste* very good. So they teamed up with an organization called Dairy Management, which is effectively a cheese lobby with a budget of around $140 million per year, and specifically spent money on trying to get Americans to *eat more cheese.*

The effort, and organization, was born out of slumping dairy sales in the face of America's recent interest in reducing the amount of saturated fat in their diets. Only a few years earlier, the organization had funded a series of studies intended to show how eating more high-fat dairy could help Americans lose weight. Of course, the science didn't support that so they simply reverted to the "but it's so delicious!" argument.

Together, Domino's and Dairy Management devised a plan to increase the amount of cheese on their pizza by around forty percent, which worked, and although the pizza became *much* worse for your health, it's continuing to sell like gangbusters.[20] The problem with that isn't that Domino's is giving America what it wants (who doesn't love cheese?); the problem is that Dairy Management is a *government-funded agency* with a vested interest in dairy-farming.

The program, which saw increased support under presidents George W. Bush and Barack Obama, spends tax payer money every year to try to convince people to eat more cheese, while other government programs work to convince you that high fat diets aren't healthy. The government is spending money to discredit *its own* efforts to make you eat better, and it could be argued that isn't even an intentional move... it's just a product of a massive government with poor internal communication and, occasionally, some pretty shady motivations. What do you think would happen if a government intentionally went out of its way to mislead you about your diet? How pervasive would that become?

By Alex Hollings

Well, let's see: do you think eating more carrots will improve your eyesight? If you said yes, maybe, or "Ya know, I've totally heard that might be true," then you know just how far a government propaganda campaign that ended more than 70 years ago can reach when it comes to what we eat.

1National Archive

Back in World War II, British (and eventually American) pilots were tasked with the near impossible feat of engaging German bombers over the English Channel under cover of darkness. At the time, aviators had to rely primarily on their own senses rather than the suite of technological gadgets we use for intercepts in modern combat, but the advent of on-board Airborne Interception Radar (AI) gave the Brits a fighting chance at locating the bombers before they could reach land. The thing is, if the Nazis were to learn about England's new plane-based radar, they would immediately begin working to subvert it... so England's Ministry of Information hatched an idea: they'd convince the world British aviators simply had incredible night vision.

Like any good disinformation campaign, they needed to find a basis in fact to use as the bedrock for their deception, and they didn't have to go far to find it – it was already growing beneath their feet.

Vitamin A has long been known to be an important part of your diet for eye health, and for those with vitamin A deficiencies, eating food rich with the vitamin can indeed improve eyesight (back to normal levels). With this in mind, the Ministry of Information looked for a food rich in Vitamin A to credit with their pilot's "incredible night vision"– carrots.

Carrots were a brilliant choice for other reasons too: the war effort had limited sugar rations throughout the country, and people were eager to find snacks they could incorporate into their kid's diets.[21] What better snack on the go than one that'll help you see during the government mandated blackouts intended to inhibit bomber targeting? By pushing carrots, the government was able to offset concerns about rationing other food stuffs, while convincing the Germans that they were shooting down their planes using nothing more than some good old-fashioned British agriculture.

The success of the campaign is difficult to measure, as it was only a matter of time before the Germans realized their enemies across the Channel were using more than good eyesight to engage their bombers. One RAF night fighter ace, John Cunningham (nicknamed "Cat's Eyes") managed to rack up 20 kills, 19 of which were at night – the Germans likely knew *something* was afoot. Nonetheless, in homes all around the world, parents still tell their kids to finish their carrots because it will improve their vision.

As a basis for comparison, that would be like if people told kids eating Vitamin C will add thirty years to their lives, simply because a serious vitamin C deficiency could cause scurvy.

Modern marketing is such an intrinsic part of our daily lives today that a campaign like that could almost certainly skew your perspective toward thinking all GMOs were harmful, for instance, or sell you on the idea that opposing political party members are freedom-hating monsters. Propaganda isn't going anywhere – if anything, it's improving all the time.

Keep that in mind the next time you're watching CNN or Fox News... and of course, don't forget to eat your carrots.

Foreign Influence Efforts Today

"Propaganda, to be effective, must be believed. To be believed, it must be credible. To be credible, it must be true."
- Hubert H. Humphrey, 38th Vice President of the United States

The 21st century has revolutionized the way in which information, and *disinformation*, can be transmitted to the masses. At its heart, propaganda is no different than marketing - both seek to influence your decisions through language and imagery. Where the two part is in intent: marketing hopes to win you over for the sake of a company or organization, propaganda seeks to win you over for the sake of a government sponsored narrative.

While propaganda and perception management campaigns are far from new, the means by which national governments can disseminate information *and disinformation* have weaponized the endeavor in entirely new ways. Online communications have eliminated many of the barriers that once existed between governments and people -- allowing state actors unprecedented access to the social communities of other nations.

Here in the United States, we've grown accustomed to being marketed to, but that cynicism toward overt messaging has not extended into our online interactions, where things like confirmation bias and our own polarized political environment incentivize seeking news you *prefer*, rather than the truth. This environment of distrust in the media has created opportunity for independent news outlets of the sort I pride myself in working for, but it has also primed the populous for a new slew of information operations tailor made for social media distribution. When you believe you can't trust the news you see on TV, it becomes easier to accept a seemingly incredible headline from a source you don't recognize.

Because we don't know where to turn for objective, honest truth, we choose to believe that which most closely reflects our own beliefs, supports our sense of identity, or confirms our fears about the proverbial "other."

The following stories all pertain to modern efforts to skew the perspectives of Americans, born outside of our borders. These efforts come with a wide array of motives, ranging from general discord to adjusting the ways in which Americans view foreign government.

Some nations, like Russia, do so by engaging with Americans directly over the internet, while others, like China, do so through purchased influence in the private sector. Even nations with few fewer resources that those two propaganda power houses like North Korea have begun learning to take their cues from their neighbors in Russia and China -- working to shape the narrative associated with their pursuit of nuclear weapons.

Organizing events through social media in foreign countries, funding Hollywood blockbusters, or acting the part of the bullied nuclear power -- perception management campaigns on the global stage now have more reach, and more power, than in any era of human history.

Propaganda is everywhere: Why Americans are susceptible to Russian meddling

Thanks to the ongoing investigation into Russian meddling into the 2016 presidential election, there's been an increased focus on just how things like social media can be used to affect the mindset of your average American voter. While some have taken a decisive stand regarding the subject, stating outright that foreign efforts to influence an election cannot be tolerated, there's still been a sizable contingent of Americans keen to dismiss Russia's underhanded foreign policy, citing the fact that Russian influencers didn't *actually change any votes*, but rather just worked to influence Americans – after all, we're all reasonable, intelligent adults that should be able to tell the difference between *real* and *fake* news, right?

Whether you feel that way, or are *furious* at the Americans who do, that means the Russian influence effect is already working.

Here in the U.S., we all grow up in an advertiser's paradise. According to the American Psychological Association, the average child is exposed to upwards of 40,000 advertisements per year, each and every year of their young lives.[22] This inundation likely has a number of effects, including the overwhelming need to get this year's hot toys for Christmas, but among the others are two things that, when combined, make for a dangerous cocktail of manipulability in American adults. First, advertising clearly *works*, which is why American companies spent almost $80 billion *on digital ads alone* in 2016. The second, is that we Americans, who grow up on a steady diet of advertisements, tend to think of ourselves as pretty marketing savvy, and overestimate our ability to shrug off advertising's influence on us.

As I studied marketing and PR in graduate school, there were a number of concepts that were readily up for debate, but among them was never whether or not it *worked*. Manipulating people in the digital sphere, in particular, is still a new phenomenon, meaning there are new and creative ways to get inside someone's head discovered each day – and make no mistake about it, studying marketing and public relations is, in fact, studying ways to manipulate people's perceptions. Often, the intent is to skew consumers toward a product or service, but occasionally, its role is to skew consumers *away* from a competitor's, or simply to minimize the effect of what could be bad news for the brand.

And that's where Russian meddling comes in. The digital effort to influence America's presidential elections didn't need to include the actual manipulation of votes to be successful, because the precise number of votes was never to be the measure of success for the campaign. Ensuring a bitterly divided political environment left the United States socially crippled, however, was the intent all along – as was demonstrated by recent revelations that the Russian effort including sowing seeds of racial discord in places like Charlottesville.

Those on the Left who triumphantly point at Vladimir Putin, claiming that he and Trump are bed fellows, have missed the point by as wide a margin as those who remain unabashedly in Trump's corner regarding the influence, denying Russia could have had any effect on the conservative turnout of voters at all. In fact, the lines each group keep drawing in the sand and then daring their opposition to cross shows, better than anything, that we are all susceptible to manipulation; whether it's regarding where to buy our socks, or who we should hate on Facebook. As Americans, we've demonstrated our propensity for hating one another, and the Russian manipulation machine is aware of it. They didn't have to invent discord, they just needed to encourage it.

One common method of marketing that we all tend to think we're too smart to get tricked by is repetition. When you hear an ad repeat the product's name ten times in sixty seconds, using the same tone and inflection, you ignore it, or maybe roll your eyes at their inability to come up with something more creative for their 60-second Super Bowl spot. The thing is, repetition is statistically proven to affect many consumer's purchasing decisions – and advertising professionals work tirelessly to find the "effective frequency" a logo must be shown or a name must be repeated in order to have the maximum possible effect on the consumer.

Study this stuff for a little while and the world begins to look a whole lot more devious to you. Eventually you come to realize that diamond engagement rings are a fairly recent development born out of a De Beers marketing campaign (they even introduced the traditional "2 months' salary" quota for the rings), or that women, by and large, didn't shave their armpits until Gillette started marketing the idea that female armpit hair was unsavory in the early twentieth century. Even grocery stores utilize a careful combination of layout, visual cues, and product placement to encourage you to buy *more* and when you do, to *choose the more expensive options* – ya know, the same basic mindset employed by casinos to keep you gambling.

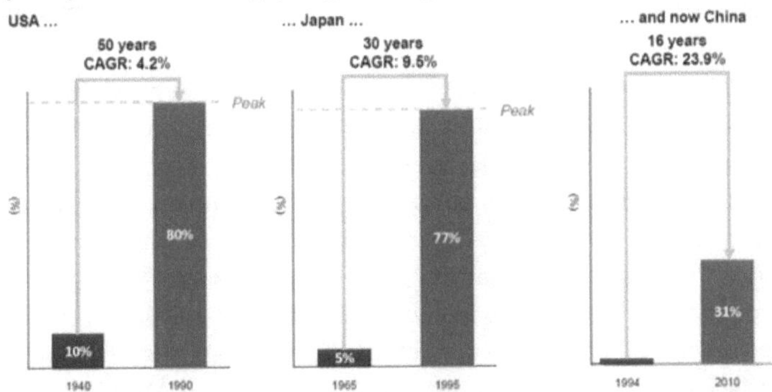

De Beers created this graph to measure how effective their ad campaigns were as they ran in each country, starting with America.

Note, the push to make engagement rings a tradition in China only recently began, thanks to De Beers.

The whole world out there is designed to manipulate you, and in a thousand ways a day, *it does.* For many of us, that manipulation comes in the form of confirmation bias, where we choose to believe the details or presentation of a story that already jives with our world view, rather than that which does not. The aforementioned repetition method, combined with something called "source amnesia" (wherein you remember a fact but not where you heard it) creates a blurry line between *knowing* something for sure, and just *hearing something often enough* to think you know it.

Foreign governments aren't just hearing about the immense power marketing has over people now – no, it's in the news because *we're* paying attention now. As mentioned before, countless things throughout modern history have been the product of public manipulation campaigns, and Russia is no newcomer to the concept. Stories about Rasputin's death being supernatural were conjured up to increase the prominence of those who took responsibility for his death. The KGB intentionally planted ideas in media outlets about the CIA planning Kennedy's assassination and many Americans continue to adhere to those theories to this day, not to mention the idea that HIV was invented as a weapon to target gays and minorities. The list goes on and on.

It's tempting to take offense when someone suggests the Russians conspired to help the politician you voted for take office. For many, it feels almost like being accused of helping the Russians yourself, but those accusations are an abbreviation of the subject so egregious that they've shed away the reality of public perception manipulation efforts. As we've discussed regarding other topics, overt propaganda rarely works as well in this day in age – we're all just a little too cynical to be *told* what to do – but soft efforts, like bolstering the voice of an outspoken minority group, whether that's ANTIFA or White Nationalists, or helping to advance a false narrative about a politician, like Pizza Gate, is really all it takes to start *creating* a narrative where one didn't previously exist.[23]

Here in America, we're all just about certain now that our news outlets are trying to manipulate us. Whether you prefer CNN or Fox, you're often sure that the other is out to ruin America, and are usually even willing to admit that your own outlet occasionally misconstrues things to support their political angle. What we often don't realize, however, is that our world is *chock full* of that same kind of manipulation, whether it's to sell you a mattress or get you to vote for Hillary Clinton. Russian efforts to shift your perception, like the efforts of the Chinese and countless other nations, wouldn't stop if we all deleted Facebook. They continue, in various forms, because they're effective – and will continue to be as long as we're willing to turn off our cynicism whenever we're reading, listening to, or seeing stuff we like to hear about the opposing party.

The marketing conscious life is a sort of depressing one. When you realize everything from the morning news to the supermarket you stop at on your way home are designed specifically to manipulate you, it can be easy to start to hate all of it. Some people, at this point, would probably tell you to accept this way of life, as it's the one we were born into, and to recognize that most advertising and marketing efforts are innocuous enough. Not here. Hating the ways people try to manipulate you will force you to be aware, and to quote one of the greatest pieces of anti-Russian propaganda to widely effect a generation of Americans that now face the resurgence of the Russian threat... The hate keeps me warm.

By Alex Hollings

Op-Ed: Celebrity fools... or traitors? When Hollywood's elite go to work for dictators

Each presidential election year, a slew of celebrities come out in support of their candidate of choice, drawing attention to their political causes from some, and harsh criticism from others. Without exception, each celebrity political endorsement eventually leads to a single argument, however: why should we care what some actor thinks?

Despite the inherent logic to that argument, it's clear that, in the modern world, *lots* of people care what celebrities think. Reality television, ironic as the name might be, exists almost entirely as a means for Americans to get a peek behind the curtain, and learn more about some of the faces we've been watching on TV and in movies: "Celebrity Rehab," "Dancing with the Stars," "The Apprentice"... all just a thin veneer over an age-old product: celebrity.

The problem with how much influence we allow our stars to exercise over the public, of course, is that celebrities are fallible human beings just like the rest of us. In fact, the bubble of constant approval most famous people find themselves living inside may even make them more susceptible to the influence of powerful foreign leaders (or religious ones, for that matter). Men like Vladimir Putin, for instance, with an extensive career in Russia's FSB (successor to the KGB), are well suited to manipulating the air of importance an audience with him can provide, in order to sell a celebrity on what an association with him could offer in terms of legitimacy.

Dennis Rodman, as a great example, saw his memory as the weirdest NBA player of all time and occasional Van Dam sidekick dwindling... but has enjoyed a resurgence in name recognition and apparent moral superiority since becoming BFF's with North Korean despot, Kim Jong Un. For many celebrities, these relationships with foreign leaders offer them the opportunity to step back into the spotlight, to be taken seriously for once... but most of all, these relationships come with money, either directly, or through endorsements.

We all know about Dennis Rodman's repeated trips to North Korea. Rodman claims Kim Jong Un seems like a generally great guy, while refusing to address or acknowledge the human rights abuses that take place within North Korea's closed borders, claiming torture and starvation falls just outside his purview as a "basketball ambassador." Of course, he simultaneously claims that international diplomacy somehow falls within that same scope... not unlike Jane Fonda, who famously shucks responsibility for her own actions during the Vietnam War, while taking credit for opposing the war effort itself.

But what about other, lesser known celebrity endorsers of tyrants, dictators, and enemies of the United States? You may be surprised to learn that the list doesn't only include washed-up has beens... but there are certainly a fair share of them on the list.

Fred Durst.

As SOFREP has reported before, Fred Durst made his way into the Russian misinformation machine rather organically: by chasing a paycheck. When the rap-metal pioneer who rose to fame by spouting lyrics like, "I did it all for the nookie, so you can take that cookie, and stick it up you're a**," managed to get his band back together in 2009, he was disappointed to learn that no one in the United States cared. This left Durst in a tough spot: if he was hoping to go on tour to solve his money woes, but no one in America was interested in seeing them perform... where else could they go on tour?

It turns out, one of the few places left on the planet that might be excited to see Fred Durst get out of breath while rapping George Michael lyrics was, you guessed it, Russia. During Durst's multiple Russian tours in recent years, Russia annexed Crimea (2014) and began efforts to shape the narrative around their violations of international law. Part of that campaign included finding celebrity spokespeople for their newly acquired territory:

Russian Embassy, UK ✔
@RussianEmbassy

.@FredDurst of @LimpBizkit says he wants to live in Crimea – welcome!

10:50 AM - 8 Oct 2015

187   84

Durst promptly moved to Russian-controlled Crimea, with his new Russian wife, and set about producing Russian-funded films that demonstrate the "great future of Crimea and Russia."

Jackie Chan

Jackie Chan rose to prominence in American cinema thanks to his brutal action sequences that often involved Chan himself accomplishing (or sometimes failing to accomplish) incredible feats of strength and coordination. Chan reinvigorated the martial arts genre with films like "Rumble in the Bronx," and then demonstrated his physical comedy chops in flicks like "Drunken Master." Jackie Chan represented a bridge between Chinese and American film culture that could be credited with helping to grow the now-massive Chinese film market.

He's also a Communist propagandist who produces Chinese films aimed at exercising influence over foreign markets... and that's not a slanderous observation made up in the SOFREP editorial offices, it's a direct quote from accusations levied at Chan from within his own nation. When not marketing films to U.S. audiences, he's talking about how China's woes are not only the fault of the United States... but also, because he thinks the Chinese populous has "too much freedom."

I'm not sure if it's good to have freedom or not," Chan said to a crowd of people during his tour for the movie, "Warcraft."[24]

"I'm really confused now. If you're too free, you're like the way Hong Kong is now. It's very chaotic. Taiwan is also chaotic. I'm gradually beginning to feel that we Chinese need to be controlled. If we're not being controlled, we'll just do what we want."

For his efforts to further the causes of the Chinese Government, they made him a national-level delegate of the Chinese People's Political Consultative Conference in 2013, one of the country's most prominent political advisory bodies.

Steven Seagal

Like Jackie Chan, Steven Seagal earned his place in VHS collections all over the United States in martial arts films, though his movies often depicted Seagal in roles like Navy SEAL, secret ninja policeman, or Secret Ninja Navy SEAL. Despite the man's affinity for Asian culture sometimes resulting in what may be among the earliest known public displays of what would one day be called "cultural appropriation," there seemed little question that Seagal was an American and a patriot. Hell, in 1998, he made a movie simply called, "The Patriot."

But in the years since, even Seagal's attempts at retaining his fame by way of going into real (fake) televised law enforcement began to fail, and the man needed to find a new way to remain relevant. Fortunately for him, the same military annexation of Crimea in 2014, and the same Russian-led effort to find celebrity endorsers for war crimes that gave Durst's career a resurgence, came through for Seagal as well.

Seagal even went so far as to call the military annexation of Crimea, which has led to a formidable standoff in the region between Russian and NATO forces, "very reasonable."

Recently, Seagal became a full-fledged Russian citizen, though he has taken the time to chime in on American politics nonetheless, publicly calling the NFL protests "disgusting," despite doing so with a Russian passport, via Russian television, in a segment filmed in Russia… where he lives. Regardless of where you stand on the topic of NFL protests, you have to appreciate the irony there.

Everybody partied with Gaddafi

It isn't at all uncommon for celebrities, especially singers, to accept huge paydays to perform at private functions for powerful people. Often, these celebrities claim ignorance when confronted with questions about why they'd feel it was appropriate for them to sing and dance for foreign leaders that have been accused of crimes against humanity, and in some cases, those claims seem founded. When footage of Jennifer Lopez singing "Happy Birthday" to Turkmenistan President Gurbanguly Berdymukhamedov, a man frequently accused of heading one of the most oppressive regimes in the world, she admitted that she was paid to perform at a private show that she didn't even know was sponsored by the Turkmenistan government. Admittedly, most people would have to google Turkmenistan to find out where it is on a map, so one could almost excuse Miss Lopez of being ignorant of the nation's politics.

But what about when celebrities accept huge cash payouts to perform for men internationally recognized as despots and tyrants? In that category, few men were more internationally renowned than Libyan dictator Muammar Gaddafi before his death. Beyoncé, Usher, Nelly Furtado, 50 Cent and Mariah Carey are just some of the singers that were paid up to a million dollars apiece to perform at parties for the Gaddafi family.

When their massive payouts from the dictator were made public, Beyoncé and Furtado both publicly donated their paychecks to charity and the American media promptly forgot all about it – because Gaddafi may have been a dictator, but Beyoncé is a queen.

By Alex Hollings

RUSSIAN EFFORTS

By Alex Hollings

Russia accuses US of committing hostile act for easing restrictions on arming rebels

Although the Syrian government has reclaimed the embattled city of Aleppo, civil war within the nation is far from over. On Christmas Eve, Russian airstrikes against several towns in rebel-held areas of the country were said to have injured and killed civilians, as reported by the U.S.-backed opposition group forced out of the city two days prior. Now, Russia has accused the United States of committing a "hostile act" by easing restrictions on arming the Syrian rebels.

Departing President Barack Obama signed the annual defense policy bill into law last week, which included language permitting the United States to send surface-to-air missiles to rebel groups in Syria. Russian foreign ministry spokeswoman Maria Zakharova called the policy change a hostile act, and suggested that the weapons would soon end up "in the hands of jihadists with whom the sham 'moderate' opposition have long acted jointly."

"Such a decision is a direct threat to the Russian air force, to other Russian military personnel, and to our embassy in Syria, which has come under fire more than once. We therefore view the step as a hostile one," Zakharova said in a statement from Moscow.

President Obama and other U.S. officials have been extremely critical of Russian airstrikes in support of Syrian President Bashar al-Assad's regime. The Obama administration recently expanded the list of Russians subjected to sanctions as a result of Russia's military annexation of Crimea in 2014, and American Ambassador to the U.N. Samantha Power recently asked Russia and its allies in Syria if they were "incapable of shame" regarding their actions in Aleppo. Russia and Iran both assisted the Syrian regime in retaking portions of the city that had been held by rebels.

In a separate statement, Zakharova addressed the increased sanctions imposed by the Obama administration by suggesting that Russia would respond in due time.[25]

"It is high time for Washington to understand that these attempts are futile and doomed to fail, and that the new restrictions, naturally, will not go unanswered. We will decide the specific type, time, and scope of our response."

Russia doubled down on their idea that weapons provided to Syrian rebels would quickly fall into the hands of terrorists and jihadis, going so far as to suggest that the U.S.-backed rebels aren't any different from the pockets of ISIS fighters both U.S. and Russian forces have taken military action against in Syria over the past year.

"Washington has placed its bets on supplying military aid to anti-government forces who don't differ than much from bloodthirsty head-choppers. Now, the possibility of supplying them with weapons, including mobile anti-aircraft complexes, has been written into this new bill," Zakharova said in her statement.

As President Obama's time in office comes to an end, some Russians have accused him of trying to ensure tensions remain high between the two nations. Trump called for normalized relations between Russia and the United States throughout his campaign, and American intelligence agencies have announced with some level of certainty that Russian hackers attempted to discredit Democrat candidate Hillary Clinton in her campaign against Trump. This level of friendly discourse could be attributed to Russia's desire to have sanctions against it eased, but many in both parties have grown uneasy with the president-elect's seemingly friendly demeanor toward Russian President Vladimir Putin.

Only time will tell if the new policy stipulations will result in more weapons being delivered to Syrian rebels, or if Trump's administration will opt not to continue to support rebel forces in the region at all. One thing is certain: On January 20th, the population of both nations will be eager to see what direction the new president will take Russian-American relations, and how it will affect nations like Syria that find themselves caught in the balance.

State-owned Russian tank maker publishes propaganda for preschoolers

One of Russia's largest state-owned weapons producers is set to release a children's book aimed at preschoolers about a little tank that learns about the "adventures" of Russian weapon systems in "foreign lands."[26]

The book, entitled, "Adventures of the Little Tank," follows a toy that was accidentally left in a museum full of Russian weapon platforms produced by the defense company, Uralvagonzavod. It follows the little tank as it meets the full-sized machines and hears tales of the things they've done throughout the world. Among the vehicles the little tank meets are the Soviet World War II era T-34 as well as a modern Armata tank. Each tank tells a story to the little "adventurer" about its exploits in combat and is accompanied by exercises such as pages to color or word searches.[27]

According to the company, Russian author Svetlana Lavrova "tells pre-school children about awe-inspiring combat vehicles in an accessible and absorbing way." They added that the book is intended to instill patriotism in Russian children while encouraging them to pursue interests in engineering.

Uralvagonzavod has been developing and producing combat vehicles for the Russian state for eighty years, and this isn't their first attempt at spreading their message of Russia's combat escapades to children. Another book aimed at teenagers has already been released, though it drew less concern because of its target audience's older age. It is styled more like an encyclopedia that features a wide variety of combat vehicles and provides information regarding each one.

This move has been compared to another Russian company's recent decision to sell cots shaped like the Buk missile launcher system that shot down Malaysia Airlines flight MH17 with 298 people on board. The cot went on sale in October and garnered quite a bit of criticism in both international and domestic media.[28]

Russia rejected the results of a Dutch led investigation that concluded that Russian forces fired the missile that killed everyone on board the flight, and Russian Foreign Minister Sergei Lavrov refused to apologize for the incident, suggesting that the investigators were unable to concretely establish who fired the weapon.

CaroBus, the company that produces and sells the bed, responded to criticisms by changing the bed's name to "Defender." It also released a statement that read, "We draw your attention to the fact that this is a defensive weapon, not an offensive one. It has been guarding the peace in the skies since 1980."

It may be more difficult for Uralvagonzavod to argue that their "little tank" and his lessons about Russian military operations in "foreign lands" is meant to emphasize peace. Russia is obviously not the first or only nation accused of targeting children with military propaganda. Governments have always aimed to persuade their citizens into supporting war efforts when necessary, and those efforts have often extended to children. However, war propaganda is traditionally reserved for times of war, and Russian involvement in Syria's civil strife notwithstanding, Russia is not currently entangled in a fight that might warrant such an effort. Instead, this move may indicate a shift in Russian perceptions about the world at large, and an anticipation of wars to come.

This perceptual prophecy could be self-fulfilling as tensions rise between Russia and NATO in the years to come.

How Fred Durst became a tool for Russian propaganda

1997 was a great year for movies. Titanic, Men in Black, The Fifth Element, and even a Jurassic Park sequel that made a little bit of sense took the world by storm, and although Pierce Brosnan set out to make James Bond as lame as he could (again), Harrison Ford played an American president that threw Gary Oldman off of a plane. In a cinematic sense, the world was as it should be for the most part... but music was another story.

The same year that brought us Will Smith welcoming aliens to earth also brought about the mainstream adoption of rap metal... and bands like Limp Bizkit, fronted by a guy that looks exactly like every guy you went to high school with that lived in a trailer park (I lived in one too, so I'm allowed to say that). Fred Durst made millions with lyrics like, "Hey I think about the day/My girlie ran away with my pay/When fellas come to play" and effectively made it impossible for people of my generation to ever claim that "music had substance back in my day."

In the years since, the musical world left Durst and his poetic lyrics behind in favor of new weirdos with even stranger things to say, and we've been blessed by the absence of his flat brimmed hat-wearing antics... but that's not the end of Durst's, or Limp Bizkit's, story.

In 2009, the band decided to get back together despite no one knowing or caring that they had broken up. They chose Russia to launch their new tour, which Durst claims was because the American public always misunderstood his lyrics and didn't appreciate the real emotion behind his work. In fairness to Durst, I'll post some of those easily misunderstood lyrics here:

I did it all for the nookie
C'mon
The nookie
C'mon
So you can take that cookie
And stick it up your, yeah!!
Stick it up your, yeah!!
Stick it up your, yeah!!"

My keenly-tuned pop-culture brain feels like the problem with launching a Limp Bizkit U.S. tour in 2009 probably had more to do with the fact that the band had already been a joke for the better part of a decade and not even a hot new jam about doing things for nookie could squeeze another dollar out of the American public... but I'll give the artist the benefit of the doubt.

Limp Bizkit continues to play in Russia, taking advantage of the language barrier (I assume) to go on subsequent Russian tours in 2012 and 2013 – as well another one at the end of last year. Between the 2013 and the 2016 tours however, a different thing was all the rage within the Russian state: the military annexation of Crimea in 2014.

While most of the world does not recognize Crimea as a part of the Russian nation, Durst certainly does – referring to the region as "Russia" in social media and claiming that he'd like to buy a house there. In fact, his claims made it all the way to the Russian embassy in the UK who were more than happy to let the world know that Russia's newest celebrity tourist destination, Crimea, was the perfect spot for American celebrities once we're done with them.

Russian Embassy, UK ✅
@RussianEmbassy

.@FredDurst of @LimpBizkit says he wants to live in Crimea – welcome!

10:50 AM - 8 Oct 2015

↩ ♺ 187   ♥ 84

Durst later went on a Russian radio program and announced that he'd like to obtain Russian citizenship and feels as though the way Russia is depicted in the American media is entirely unfair.[29] Again, demonstrating the man's inherent knack for crafting art from language, he went on to say, "I want to prove to everyone that it's really cool!"

Sputnik news, one of the many Russian owned news distributors that has weaseled its way into Western laptops, loves the singer, reporting on the band's tours, cars he uses in music videos, and Durst's wish to move to Crimea as though he's just another in a long slew of

American celebrities that are eager to make the change from Hollywood elite to military oversight in the breadlines.[30]

Russia has promised financial support for movies and music produced in Crimea and Durst recently announced that he's making the transition into directing films[31] – it must be serendipity that brought Durst's aspirations to Crimea just as Russian forces were securing it to be "the new Hollywood," right? Because by October of 2015, Durst had already petitioned the authorities in Crimea to allow him to move to the region and begin filming movies to work toward the "great future of Crimea and Russia."

Ukraine must not have gotten word about Limp Bizkit getting back together, because they promptly banned Durst from entering their nation for a minimum of five years – forfeiting their right to future tour dates and their chances to hear a forty-six-year-old man rap the lyrics to a George Michael song in person.[32]

Like so many celebrities that think the attention their name garners makes their opinions valuable, Durst is likely not aware of the reality faced by many people in Crimea. Like Tom Cruise and Scientology, or

Madonna somehow thinking it's okay to talk about blowing up the White House, living in the spotlight is no guarantee that the synapses in your brain will fire in the right order to make you aware of how dumb you look. Despite those allowances I can make on his behalf, I'd like to be the first American to say – Mr. Putin, please grant Fred Durst Russian citizenship. We don't want him, and Russian prostitutes, whom you've already claimed are the best in the world, need something other than the sound of snow falling in Siberia to dance to. America can manage without Limp Bizkit.

By Alex Hollings

White House accuses Russia of trying to 'cover up' chemical attack, Putin accuses the U.S. of planting it

While American Secretary of State Rex Tillerson visits Moscow this week, the Kremlin and the White House continue to exchange jabs in the media over the chemical weapon attack in Syria last Tuesday, and the resulting American military action taken against Assad's regime on Thursday.

White House spokesman Sean Spicer once again voiced the concerns of the Trump administration regarding Russia's seemingly unwavering support for Assad and his regime in Syria, claiming that Russia is isolating themselves from the international community by continuing to stand by the Syrian leader.

"Russia is on an island when it comes to its support of Syria," Spicer told reporters. "In this particular case, it's no question that Russia is isolated. They have aligned themselves with North Korea, Syria, Iran. That's not exactly a group of countries you're looking to hang out with. With the exception of Russia, they are all failed states."[33]

According to Spicer and other White House officials, a concerted Russian and Syrian effort to mislead the public as to the events that occurred in Syria last week is already under way, claiming the two nations are working to "confuse the world community about who is responsible for using chemical weapons against the Syrian people in this and earlier attacks."

Russian president Vladimir Putin's recent statements regarding the attack could be seen as indicative that the White House has reason to suspect a disinformation campaign is afoot, as Putin went so far as to nearly accuse the American government of having a hand in "planting" sarin gas in Syrian villages to justify taking military action against Assad, despite President Trump's announced policy shift away from removing Assad from power coming only days before the Sarin gas attack.

When asked by the Russian media about the potential for subsequent U.S. attacks against Syrian assets, Putin responded, "We have information that a similar provocation is being prepared ... in other parts of Syria including in the southern Damascus suburbs where they are planning to again plant some substance and accuse the Syrian authorities of using (chemical weapons)."

Of course, accusations of the Russians not only attempting to cover up the chemical attack after it occurred, but also of being complicit in the decision to use Sarin gas on civilians have been levied by a number of top U.S. Defense Officials and Russian military personnel have been confirmed to have been operating out of the same air base used to launch the attack.[34]

"We do think that it is a question worth asking the Russians," a senior White House official said. "How is it possible that their forces were located with the Syrian forces that planned, prepared and carried out this chemical weapons attack at the same installation, and did not have foreknowledge?"

"Russia's allegations fit with a pattern of deflecting blame from the regime and attempting to undermine the credibility of its opponents." The official added.

A White House report provided to journalists indicated that the chemical attack was delivered by Syrian Su-22 aircraft that took off from the Shayrat airfield that was targeted in Thursday's strike.[35]

"Additionally, our information indicates personnel historically associated with Syria's chemical weapons program were at Shayrat airfield in late March making preparations for an upcoming attack in northern Syria, and they were present at the airfield on the day of the attack," the report said.

President Trump chose not to comment on the possibility of Russian collusion regarding the chemical attack, though it is certainly an issue Secretary of State Rex Tillerson is expected to broach behind closed doors with his Russian counterpart this week.

Russia has requested a UN led independent investigation into the circumstances surrounding the chemical attack last week, but no official statement has been made by UN officials regarding one.

Op-Ed: Let's have a real talk about perception, comments sections, and Syria

Ah, the Facebook comments section. A place where well-informed discourse gives way to emotional rants intended to insult an author or entire site. Honestly, I don't mind it – we all need a way to blow off some steam, and not everyone shares my hobbies. For me, my punching bag is... well, a punching bag. For others, it's websites, authors, or other commenters that had the audacity to present evidence that doesn't support your position. After all, there's no way *you* could be wrong... and the world needs to know.

Despite not chiming in on random Facebook posts (or continuing to follow outlets I don't like), I'm certainly not above it. My Twitter account is primarily used as a means by which to convey short messages to the hosts of my favorite podcasts. Recently, while listening to the Cracked podcast, I was so baffled by Jack O'brien's claims that there were no liberal media outlets beating up on reasonable Republicans "as they so often claim," that I pulled my phone out of my pocket in the middle of a workout just to remind him that he's devoted countless entire podcasts to doing *just that.* In his defense, the Cracked Podcast often tries to present pretty reasonable discourse, and has never once claimed to be unbiased... and I love their work, even when I don't agree with it.

I ended up deleting the Tweet (I cringe every time I type that word) not because I felt like I was wrong, but because I noticed the army of Righters that had already descended upon his Twitter feed. I didn't want to get caught up in the unreasonable attacks levied at him for doing the same thing I do every day: trying to present my thoughts to a wide audience in a way that doesn't devolve into nit-picking and complaining. I have to assume O'brien, like so many other media personalities, eventually gives up on reading the responses to his work, throws his hands in the air with his eyes rolled as hard as he's capable of and just says, "has the world gone mad?"

Well, allow me to answer the made up question I just put in his mouth: yup. It sure as hell has.

I've been astonished to see the support Assad's Syrian regime has received on social media since Tuesday's chemical attack that produced (according to CNN's most recent tally) 86 dead bodies... 26 of whom were just kids. Now, before I go on, I know some of the folks on my side of this debate will point out that social media support for Syria is absolutely in line with Russia's normal method of enforcing their agenda through digital dumb-ery, and you're absolutely right – but I've clicked on some the accounts arguing so passionately that Assad is a peace-loving man – the Abraham Lincoln of his nation's history, fighting to re-unify his war-torn home – and to my surprise, they seem to be real-life humans, complete with dogs, spouses, and faces decidedly free of the discoloration and the foam that pours out of the mouths of those who have witnessed Assad's use of chemical weapons first hand.

See, the thing is, I'm a big believer in conflict being born not just out of the traditional philosophical "fear of the other," but also out of a fear of *discomfort*. If I made public my support of, say, Bill Cosby early into the accusations levied against him about rape, the subsequent allegations and evidence would stand to make me awfully uncomfortable with myself. It's easier, then, to just say, "fake news!" and stand by my position.

In politics, we call anyone who absorbs new information and establishes a new position a "flip flopper," because if there's one thing we apparently don't want in the person leading our nation, it's the ability to change their mind in the face of new, irrefutable evidence. If you said you didn't support atomic energy when you were twenty-three, then *God help you* if you change your mind at fifty, no matter what technological advances have been made along the way.

This isn't because we're bad people – no, not even the crazies on Facebook that think the Syrian rebels somehow managed to establish secret supply lines, research facilities and laboratories, generate the elements to produce Sarin gas, choose not to ever use it in the fight their losing, but rather store the elements (traditionally maintained separately) in an above ground warehouse surrounded by children rather than in an underground bunker... Nor are the people who claim bombing the stored, separate elements (because Sarin itself has a fairly short shelf life) could somehow mix the two in the appropriate way to instantly release a cloud of the poison in a manner that looks awfully similar to the dispersal caused by an airstrike via satellite imagery... They're not bad guys. They're people who don't want to be uncomfortable.

Whew, I guess I am pretty capable of a Facebook comment style rant. Sorry about that. For the record, I'm no expert on Sarin gas – but Dan Kaszeta, a chemical weapons specialist and managing director of Strongpoint Security is:

"All the nerve agents used in the Syrian conflict so far have been binary nerve agents," he told CNN, "which are mixed from different components within a few days of use. This is done because of the difficulties of handling agents such as Sarin, which has a very short shelf life."

"Nerve agents are the result of a very expensive, exotic, industrial chemical process — these are not something you just whip up," he added.

Charles Lister, a senior fellow at the US-based Middle East Institute made the following statement.

"Are we seriously meant to believe that the opposition has a latent chemical weapons capability, and yet somehow, it has only ever suffered the effects of its own weapons and failed to use them itself?" he said.

By Alex Hollings

"First of all, nobody in their right mind would ever store both components of a binary nerve agent in the same building. And secondly, even if they were stored together and then targeted, blowing them up would not result in any active nerve agent — it's chemically impossible," he added.

Listen, I realize that a couple of eggheads rejecting the Russian and Syrian story about Tuesday's attack doesn't mean my position couldn't possibly be wrong. Even one of those experts I so snidely cited referred to the Russian account as "highly improbable," which is admittedly allowing for the small possibility that he (and I) are wrong. Multiple investigations are ongoing, and just like the attack in 2013 most of the world is happy to lay on Assad's feet, the outcomes of each of them will be ignored by those who don't *want to believe* Assad is capable of ordering such a horrific attack, just like I would ignore any story about Dwayne Johnson being anything short of a giant charmer like I want to be when I grow up.

The point is, our discourse online may seem trivial, but like pop-culture, it traverses the gap between the digital realm and the real one by infiltrating the way we think about things. While pop-culture, like internet comments sections, is often dismissed as just the silly stuff we mentally ingest to decompress at the end of the day, the evidence shows again and again that it's that silly stuff that shapes our perceptions of the world.

Popular culture teaches those that live in urban settings that rural Southerners are uneducated racists, and it teaches people who grew up on farms that the minorities they see on "The Wire" are representative of an entire ethnicity. Pop culture taught me that the pyramids in Egypt were a beautiful and peaceful place to visit (false), that diamond engagement rings are a time-honored marital tradition (advertising campaign), and that halitosis was an actual ailment that needed to be treated (invented by a real-life Don Draper). If our concept of reality is so easily shaped by the thirty-second spots between fart jokes on "Family Guy," what do you suppose years of reading troll comments on your Facebook page will do?

It might even make you believe the Syrian rebels are gassing their own kids.

If it didn't work, there wouldn't be so much hubbub about Russian meddling in foreign elections. They aren't changing ballot counts, they're changing perceptions – and if you get the ingredients just right, that can be just as good. Get them wrong, and, well, you get Pepsi's latest advertisement that suggest exchanging cans of sugar water could bring about a new era of racial harmony.[36]

So yeah, I'm sure the folks that never bother to read the articles they complain about will chime in below this one, nit-picking whatever the title ends up being and congratulating themselves for their well thought out and thorough debunking of the first four lines they could read in the description... and I have no doubt that some others will disagree with me on SOFREP below using real information and their own experts – I'm not complaining, that's *awesome.* Discussing this sort of thing is important, and if I'm wrong, I promise I'll try my best to flip-flop like a terrible politician. All I ask in exchange is that you return the favor.

And remember that the only difference between what's real and what's not is that we have to agree on what's real. If you see a camel in the road and no one else does, the camel's in your head. If you see a war crime being committed and 90% of the world does too... maybe, just maybe, it's real.

By Alex Hollings

Russian Defense Ministry accuses US of 'pretending' to fight ISIS to sabotage Syria

Relations between the United States and Russia continued to publicly degrade on Tuesday, as a spokesman for the Russian Defense Ministry accused the United States of only *pretending* to fight the Islamic State in Iraq, while intentionally permitting their forces to funnel into Syria where they are engaged with Russian-backed Syrian forces.

"Everyone sees that the U.S.-led coalition is pretending to fight Islamic State, above all in Iraq, but continuing to allegedly fight Islamic State in Syria actively for some reason," said Major-General Igor Konashenkov, a spokesman for Russia's defense ministry.[37]

According to the Russian general, the United States began to "sharply reduce" the number of air strikes they executed against ISIS forces in Iraq in September, just as the Syrian Army, which is backed by Russian air support, began making significant strides toward retaking the Deir al-Zor province in Syria. That claimed slump in air strikes then resulted in a flow of Islamic State fighters over the Iraqi border and into the same province, bolstering the terrorist forces and slowing the Syrian/Russian offensive.

He then went on to accuse the United States of choosing to reduce their combat operations against ISIS specifically for the purpose of slowing the momentum of Bashar al-Assad's troops in Syria.

"The actions of the Pentagon and the coalition demand an explanation. Is their change of tack a desire to complicate as much as they can the Syrian army's operation, backed by the Russian air force, to take back Syrian territory to the east of the Euphrates?" asked Konashenkov.

Russian diplomats have a history of making seemingly outrageous claims about the United States and its leadership, but in what would seem to be a bit of political theater, the general went on to suggest that the decision to limit air strikes may not have been an effort to sabotage the Syrian/Russian joint effort against ISIS, but instead that it may be because America hopes to take advantage of Russia's comparative air superiority.

"Or is it an artful move to drive Islamic State terrorists out of Iraq by forcing them into Syria and into the path of the Russian air force's pinpoint bombing?"

A perusal of the U.S. Department of Defense' near daily updates on air strikes executed against the Islamic State in Iraq and Syria shows a slight downturn in the number of daily strikes when comparing September, the month in question, to August, which could be construed as a basis for Konashenkov's claims.[38] In terms of averages, however, August and September both saw U.S. forces conducting nearly 30 air strikes per day. The air strikes were dispersed differently within each month. In August, daily airstrikes often came with a higher tally, whereas September's figures seem to show fewer strikes per day on most days, with significant outliers raising the average, such as September 18th, where a whopping 94 separate air strikes were executed against 126 different targets.

It seems unlikely, of course, that the Russian spokesman took the time to tally the individual strikes, and was instead commenting on the flow of reinforcements coming from Iraq, where U.S.-backed coalition forces have been capturing the few remaining ISIS strongholds in the nation over the span of recent months.

By Alex Hollings

Russia's 'irrefutable' evidence of US support for ISIS is a poorly cropped picture of a video game

Many within the United States have focused their attention on Russia's social media based disinformation campaigns as of late. However, it's important to understand that the online effort to persuade and divide the American people throughout and after the 2016 presidential election is far from an isolated aspect of the nation's overarching foreign policy. In many ways, Russia, as well as its predecessor the Soviet Union, has long relied on managing the perceptions of the global populous regarding how they view their own government, as well as the governments of opponents like the United States.

Recently, Russia's remarks regarding the use of sanctions on North Korea to dissuade Kim's development of nuclear arms indicated that the United States, not Kim's regime, was acting as the aggressor, with Putin going so far as to say he'd like to see all sanctions levied by the U.S. and United Nations dropped. Similarly, Russian officials have accused the American military of running ISIS fighters out of Iraq and into Syria, where they serve as reinforcements against the Russian-led anti-ISIS campaign. Now, Russia has claimed to have "irrefutable" evidence that the United States is actually *assisting* ISIS fighters in Iraq and Syria by providing air support. There's just one problem... that *proof* has turned out to be an image taken from a video game.

"This is the irrefutable evidence that there is no struggle against terrorism as the whole global community believes. The US are actually covering the ISIS combat units to recover their combat capabilities, redeploy, and use them to promote the American interests in the Middle East," The Russian Foreign Ministry wrote on Twitter.[39]

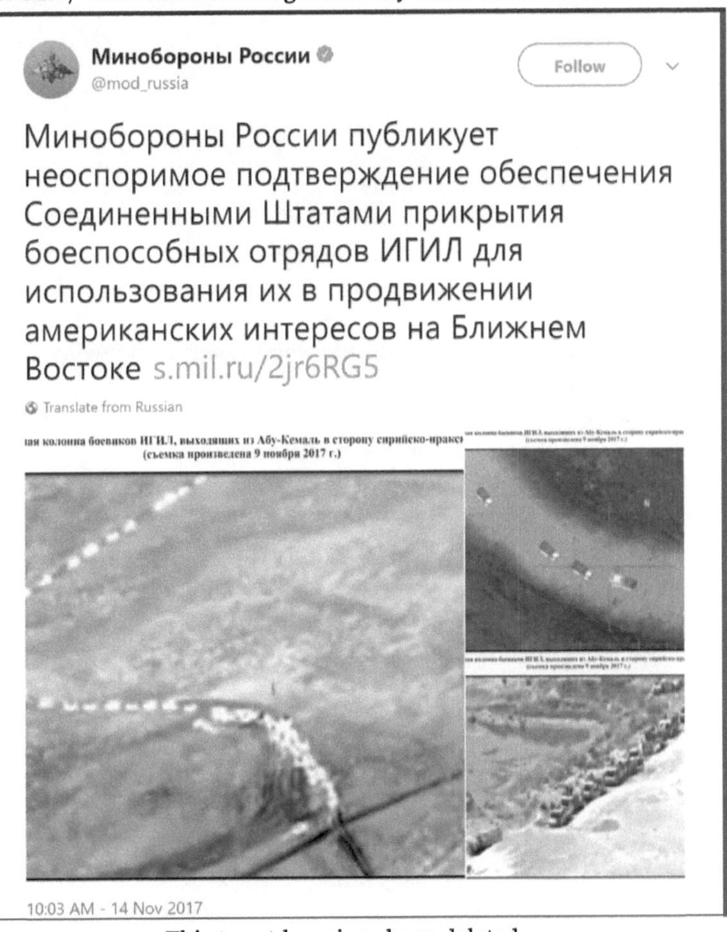

This tweet has since been deleted.

They accompanied the tweet with this image:

That image in particular caught the attention of a number of internet sleuths like Elliot Higgins, who promptly pointed out that the image is a poorly cropped shot from a YouTube video advertising a game called, "AC–130 Gunship Simulator – Convoy engagement." You can even see a portion of the disclaimer written over the YouTube footage that says, "Development footage. This is a work in progress. All content subject to change."

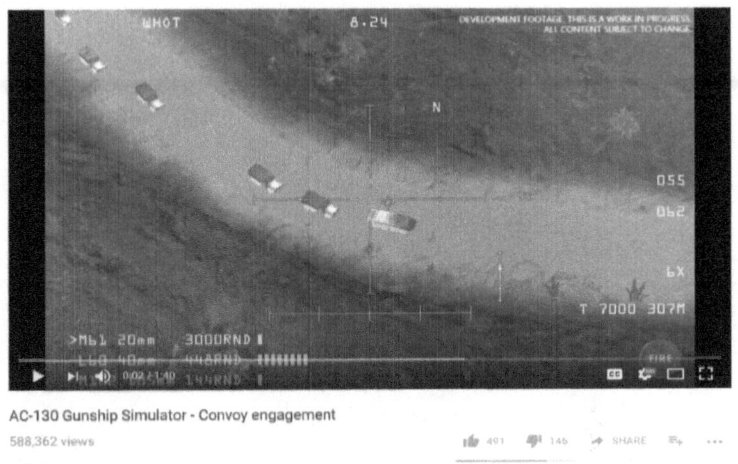

AC-130 Gunship Simulator - Convoy engagement

588,362 views

491   146   SHARE

Byte Conveyor Studios
Published on Mar 25, 2015

SUBSCRIBE 1.1K

Development preview of our upcoming game for mobile platforms, "AC-130 Gunship Simulator:

The other images included in the Russian Foreign Ministry statement also proved to be fake, though they weren't from a video game ad. They were both taken from actual combat footage out of Iraq, more than a year before the Boukamal battle Russia claimed they came from.

Russia hoped to shine a light on a deal brokered between U.S. backed Syrian forces and local tribal leaders within Syria to ferry ISIS fighters and their families out of Raqqa as it fell. A reported 50 rented trucks, 13 busses and over 100 ISIS vehicles were permitted to leave the city in late October; the BBC has reported that the U.S. coalition was aware of the permitted retreat, and even monitored it as it was underway. According to the BBC's report, which aired on Monday, as many as 250 fighters, as well as around 3,000 civilians, were permitted to flee under the agreement.

The U.S. State Department did not contest these reports, saying that the effort was not led by the Coalition but was honored by U.S. forces in order "to minimize civilian casualties in the fight that remained to liberate Raqqa."[40] With 250 fighters among 3,000 ISIS family members, it would have been near impossible to target only combatants without killing a significant number of civilians.

According to the State Department, everyone that was permitted to leave was subject to search before being released. Army Maj. Gen. James Jarrard said that under the deal brokered in Raqqa, "what we did do with the SDF, is we did take all of those [ISIS] members and we enrolled them biometrically, so that we are able to track them."

Russia, always eager to find a way to paint the United States in a negative light, could have portrayed this move as a violation of statements made by senior U.S. officials, who have made it clear on multiple occasions that their intent is to destroy ISIS and not permit any foreign fighters the opportunity to return to their native countries. U.S. reports indicate only as many as four actual ISIS fighters were permitted to leave during the brokered exodus, but local reports indicate that it was likely more.

However, by using inflammatory language and obviously faked evidence, Russia utterly undermined their position on the topic, as well as garnering a great deal of social media abuse. Twitter users have continued to send the Russian Foreign Ministry videos from video games, claiming they too have found evidence to support the Russian position, despite Russia pulling down the original post.[41]

All of which just goes to show, although Russia may have been at the misinformation game for a long time, even old pros can occasionally make mistakes.

Russia claims first interaction between F-22 and Su-35... CENTCOM calls it a fairy tale

The Russian Ministry of Defense released a barrage of statements to state-owned media outlets this week, claiming that an American F-22 fighter was chased away from Russian bombing runs in Syria by the Kremlin's advanced Su-35 fighter. There's just one problem: according to U.S. officials in CENTCOM, this first interaction between these two storied fighters never took place at all.

According to Russian officials, a single U.S. F-22 intercepted two Russian Su-25 close air support aircraft as they were conducting bombing runs on ISIS targets west of the Euphrates on November 23rd. Their statements go on to claim that the F-22 was attempting to prevent the Su-25s from continuing their runs by "simulating" a dog fight.

"The F-22 launched decoy flares and used airbrakes while constantly maneuvering [near the Russian strike jets], imitating an air fight," Major General Igor Konashenkov told the Kremlin-backed RT, an outlet that recently had to register as a foreign agent in the United States.[42] According to the general, the F-22 then broke off its engagement and ran off when the more modern Su-35s joined their older counterparts.

Per the statements of the general, the F-22's actions were "just another example" of American forces protecting ISIS militants, a claim the Kremlin has levied on a number of occasions. Recently, the Kremlin released a video they claimed "proved" the U.S. was working to support ISIS in Syria, only to have the footage exposed as fake almost immediately.

The general claimed that "most close-midair encounters between Russian and US jets in the area around the Euphrates River have been linked to the attempts of U.S. aircraft to get in the way [of the Russian warplanes] striking against Islamic State terrorists."

There has been a great deal of speculation regarding how the Su-35, a heavily updated and extremely maneuverable fighter, would fare against the stealth F-22. Although the F-35 is often touted as the most advanced combat aircraft in the world, there's little question that the F-22 is a more competent dog fighter, as the slower F-35 relies on engaging targets from a greater distance. This interaction, however brief, would have been the first time these legendary aircraft met in the air – and Syria has already been the scene of more than one air-to-air encounter involving American fighters. In June, a U.S. Navy F-18 Super Hornet shot down a Syrian Su-22 jet, which is a predecessor to the Su-35. American jets have also shot down drones over Syria on more than one occasion.

However, according to U.S. officials, the Russian account of this historic interaction is entirely *false*. Further, the CENTCOM statement refutes the idea that an American aircraft would cross the Euphrates without first deconflicting with Russian officials. However, they do go on to point out that on the same day of the Russian's claims of air superiority, Russians crossed over the deconfliction line *nine times* without once making contact with Coalition officials. The CENTCOM statement reads:

There is no truth to this allegation. According to our flight logs for Nov 23, 2017, this alleged incident did not take place, nor has there been any instance where a Coalition aircraft crossed the river without first deconflicting with the Russians via the deconfliction phone line set up for this purpose. Of note, on Nov 23, 2017, there were approximately nine instances where Russian fighter aircraft crossed to the east side of the Euphrates River into Coalition airspace without first using the deconfliction phone. This random and unprofessional activity placed Coalition and Russian aircrew at risk, as well as jeopardizing Coalition ability to support partner ground forces in the area.

Any claims that the Coalition would protect Daesh, or hinder, a strike against Daesh are completely false. We strike them hard wherever they are found. What we can tell you is that we actively deconflict the airspace in Syria with the Russians to ensure the enduring defeat of Daesh in the region. We will continue to work with our SDF partners, just as we will continue to deconflict with the Russians for future Coalition strikes against Daesh targets in Syria."[43]

By Alex Hollings

These are the 3 tenants of Russia's ongoing cyber campaigns in the United States

According to multiple sources, including Secretary of State under Donald Trump, Rex Tillerson, the Kremlin's varied digital campaign against the United States remains ongoing. While the topic has become a politically charged one within the United States, the informed debate is not about whether or not Russia has worked to manipulate events within the country, but rather, to what extent have they been successful.

While Russia's cyber warfare apparatus employs a broad spectrum of methodologies, many of their efforts can be sorted into one of three categories:

Political Manipulation

Headlines following the 2016 presidential election about the possibility of Trump colluding with the Russian government to win the election created a polarized political atmosphere. Like Benghazi for the previous administration, the shadow of potential fault loomed so large overhead that some within the political debate lost track of the original issue in favor of partisan bickering. Those with their eye on the ball, however, have already begun seeing the same influence campaign at work leading up to midterm elections next year.

In an interview with Fox News earlier this week, Tillerson explained that the United States is still in no position to stop Russian meddling with the democratic election process.

"I don't know that I would say we are better prepared, because the Russians will adapt as well," he said comparing the 2016 election to the upcoming 2018 cycle. "The point is, if it's their intention to interfere, they are going to find ways to do that. We can take steps we can take but this is something that, once they decide they are going to do it, it's very difficult to preempt it."[44]

Russia hasn't only been meddling with election-level politics, however. Facebook recently announced that an internal investigation found that Russian troll accounts shared a variety of politically fueled content aimed at both the Right and Left. Sponsored content helped ensure a wide reach, and some 62,500 users even agreed to attend political events *invented* by Russian trolls, with the intent of sowing political and sometimes racial discord within the nation.

For instance, one group of Russian based trolls created a Right-targeted protest event called, "Stop Islamization of Texas" to be held at the opening of a library at an Islamic Center on May 21, 2016. That same group of trolls then also organized a *counter* protest called "Save Islamic Knowledge," to be held at the same time, on the same date, and in the same location.[45]

Either Russia's troll army has conflicting views of Islam, or their intent was to incite conflict, be it political or physical, in Houston, Texas that day. While Russia has been painted as a Trump supporting foreign power by much of the media, their real goal could be more accurately described as political turmoil, rather than playing favorites.

Cyber Espionage

Russia tends not to be the first nation that comes to mind when addressing concerns about spying and classified military projects. That distinction is usually reserved for China, thanks to their theft and subsequent appropriation of plans for America's 5th generation fighter platforms, the F-22 and F-35. However, an Associated Press investigation released on Wednesday appears to show that Russian efforts go far beyond simply trying to manipulate the volatile political atmosphere in the U.S. The Russian hacker group known as "Fancy Bear," who first drew headlines for their involvement in trying to manipulate the 2016 presidential election, have now been implicated in an attempt to gain access to classified government projects by targeting at least 87 government contractors with an e-mail phishing scam.

The Russian effort was apparently intended to gain access to classified materials housed with Lockheed Martin, Raytheon, Boeing, Airbus, and General Atomics, among others.

"The programs that they appear to target and the people who work on those programs are some of the most forward-leaning, advanced technologies," said Charles Sowell, a former senior adviser to the U.S. Office of the Director of National Intelligence, after he reviewed the list of names for the AP. "And if those programs are compromised in any way, then our competitive advantage and our defense is compromised."[46]

Among the projects Russia attempted to gain access to was the Air Force's secretive X-37B – an orbital drone that remains in space for hundreds of days at a time, though the government remains tight lipped about what it could potentially be doing up there. There has been a growing concern about America falling behind in the militarization of orbital assets, and it would appear that Russia wants to know exactly what America's capabilities in space truly are.

Propaganda and Disinformation

There are a number of well informed discussions about Russia's massive disinformation methodologies employed in both domestic and global politics. Russia employs multiple strategies that sometimes overlap or directly contradict one another, though that in itself is a method of creating informational confusion, prompting the average spectator to lean further into their own confirmation bias. In effect, by saying all sorts of things all the time, the Russian government can get away with saying *anything* at *any time*.

Like Russia's most recent claims that their downed Su-25 pilot in Syria opted to blow himself up with a grenade rather than be captured by rebels, the Kremlin is aware of how far detached from these events most of the world's populous truly are. That gives Russia the opportunity to shape the narrative as it's presented to the world, and leaves very little opportunity to formally discredit their claims. Some other examples of Russian disinformation to come out of Syria alone include the use of stolen video game footage as alleged "evidence" of American support of the terrorist organization ISIS within Syrian borders, and the entirely fictional account of an interaction between a single American F-22 (perhaps the most capable fighter on the planet) and a Russian Su-35 (a worthy opponent), only days before a *real* intercept took place, and went nothing at all like their claims.

In both instances and a number of others, Russian officials were caught lying in formal statements released through Kremlin-owned outlets, and time and time again, these lies are glossed over in a media climate devoted to the next breaking story, rather than to follow ups or corrections on old ones.

Conclusion

The greatest success Russia has managed (perhaps unintentionally) has been the politicization of the concept of Russian manipulation. Republicans, frustrated with the Left's seeming unwillingness to even entertain Trump's presidency, often shrug off concerns about Russian influence because of the inferred complicity of their candidate in liberal leaning media. Likewise, the focal point for Democrats is often finding any thread they may be able to pull that leads to an impeachment of the president, rather than the ongoing threat presented by Russian efforts. LIke organizing both a protest *and* a counter protest at the same location, Russia's efforts are not based on choosing a political side in America's government, they're self serving. As long as Americans are entrenched in ideological warfare with one another, their position in the world continues to weaken.

By Alex Hollings

CHINESE EFFORTS

By Alex Hollings

China expands its influence in Hollywood... and why that's bad news for America

Paramount Pictures announced a new partnership with two Chinese firms worth a reported $1 billion on Friday.[47] The deal demonstrates Hollywood's continued efforts to make profitable films for both domestic and Chinese viewers, as China represents the second largest movie market on the planet.

It also means China just bought an even larger say in how the world is depicted in American films.

Whereas America utilizes a film rating system in the form of the MPAA (an honestly discriminatory and broken system, but one that isn't state owned) China utilizes government censors to determine what films are suitable to be shown in theaters across their nation. Chinese officials can ban a film for any number of reasons, but prominent among them is if they don't like the way China is being depicted in the story. Studios have long been aware of this, and it's already started to shape the films we watch.

"Iron Man 3" was meant to introduce one of Iron Man's greatest foes: the Mandarin, but concerns about Chinese censors resulted in the studio choosing Sir Ben Kingsley to play the traditionally Chinese villain, and significant re-writes regarding the character itself (I'll spare you the spoilers, but comic book nerds know what I'm talking about).[48]

The 2012 remake of "Red Dawn" was actually filmed in its entirety using China as the movie's primary antagonist, but when it became apparent that the Chinese government wouldn't permit the movie to be released within their borders, the studios went back and digitally altered every flag to add North Korean insignias, and used voice overs to change any references to China.[49]

"Pixels," a movie both Adam Sandler and I would like to forget, was originally scripted to include a scene that destroyed the Great Wall of China, but again, issues with Chinese censors led to the scene being omitted. The Chinese government saw the scene as depicting China as week, despite numerous other landmarks in other nations being destroyed throughout the film.

Most recently, Marvel's "Doctor Strange" forced the studio to take yet another large departure from Marvel's source material by moving the location of Strange's spiritual training from Tibet to Nepal. Marvel did not want to incite China's censors to block the film due to questions regarding the sovereignty of Tibet – they also cast a white woman as the traditionally Tibetan character of "The Ancient One," prompting a backlash among many in the Asian community for "white-washing" the film.

These examples, though far from exhaustive, demonstrate Hollywood's fear of Chinese censors preventing movies from reaching their markets, but I can imagine that many of you might be thinking, "so what?" None of the changes were particularly dramatic and one could argue that China has every right to exercise any influence they can on the films they permit to be released within their borders... but my background is in studying mass communications, and I can assure you that American culture will inevitably be affected by the forcefully positive depictions of China we'll see in the films Hollywood produces.

"Prove it," I can hear you shouting at your computer screen (or book as the case seems to be) – so allow me to give you a few examples of things we see as simply inherent to American or Western culture that you may not realize were actually the products of marketing and *popular* culture.

Most women in the United States devote a fair amount of time and effort to removing body hair, but a good number of us may be surprised to learn that shaving your legs and armpits wasn't a real sticking point for Americans until after World War I.[50] The fashion of the day simply didn't call for much of the female anatomy to be exposed to the public, so women weren't particularly concerned with how hairy their hidden parts remained – that is, until advertisements started surfacing in magazines like *Harper's Bazaar*, depicting models with *hairless armpits*. Suddenly it was all the rage, and the stars of the time embraced it as a means to accentuate their femininity... fast forward a few decades, and we all simply accept it as a part of life.

You know how you simply cannot get engaged without picking out the right diamond ring for your spouse to be? Yup, pop culture got you again. Up until the 1930s, the idea of exchanging a diamond to represent your impending marriage wasn't a common one at all.[51] But a few decades prior, South Africa–based cartel, De Beers Consolidated Mines, Ltd. (now De Beers) discovered a giant diamond mine. In 1938, Harry Oppenheimer, the De Beers founder's son, hired a New York–based ad agency called N.W. Ayer to promote the use of diamonds in engagement rings in every way that he could: including integrated advertising in popular culture.

The world we live in is directly shaped by the culture we consume, and that's far from a contemporary issue. The color blue was never referenced in ancient writings we're aware of.[52] In "The Odyssey," Homer refers to the color of sea as "wine-dark." Why? Because blue hadn't been invented yet. There was no word for the color in ancient Greek, Chinese, Japanese or Hebrew. This has prompted a debate among scientists and scholars as to whether or not our ancestors even *saw* blue – if their perception of the world was so intrinsically tied to language that their brains simply made the ocean appear to be the color of wine, because it's what our highly-advanced monkey brains could make sense of.[53]

I have a bit of trouble wrapping my own monkey brain around the concept, but as I've said here before, I'm rarely the smartest guy in the room.

So what does this tell us about China's influence on the movie industry? To be succinct, it means we'll likely see a new generation of Americans that think of China as much cleaner, fairer in rule, militarily powerful and all around good guys in the future. Even those of us old enough to spot propaganda when we see it rarely consider how a passing shot of Shanghai rooftops could affect how we think of China, but that didn't stop Chinese investors from forcing Mission Impossible 3 to change just such a scene because it clearly showed people using clothes lines to dry their clothes in the city. Is it accurate that most Chinese families don't have access to washers and dryers even in their skyscraper homes? Yes. Is China willing to allow that to be shown in an American film? No. And that concerns me.

As China invests billions into defense, growing their military and the influence it expends in the South China Sea and elsewhere, Chinese investments are also working to shape the way we *think* of their nation. From an academic standpoint, I have to applaud their tenaciousness. From an American perspective... I have to worry. Especially when they throw a billion dollars toward producing the movies that are already influenced by Chinese censors.

So when our culture had no word for blue, we may not have actually been able to see it as it was, even right in front of our faces... I ask, if we're no longer able to control how we depict China in one of our largest pop-culture arenas, will we see China coming as it will be, even when it's right in front of ours?

By Alex Hollings

China offers cash payouts for turning in 'suspicious foreigners'

Within the international intelligence community, China is a name that comes up pretty often. With confirmed cases of Chinese espionage resulting in state secrets migrating their way East into projects like the Chinese J-20 (which bears more than a striking resemblance to the American F-22) mentions of the economic powerhouse are often coupled with strategies intended to curb their abilities to infiltrate our national security infrastructure. Because of China's huge population and comparatively large intelligence apparatus, methods don't often even have to be that *good* in order to be employed – just ask the SOFREP writers that have been approached by Chinese intelligence gatherers in bars in Las Vegas.[54]

China has an illustrious history of successfully gaining intelligence from Western nations and employing it for their own military gain, but like any nation with offensive espionage operations underway, there's still the other side of the coin to worry about: how do you stop opposing nations from doing the same to you?

You could rely on your citizen's sense of patriotism to encourage them to turn potential spies in – but in today's global culture, it has become increasingly difficult to create the allure of nationalist idealism in enough people to make such a system aggressively effective. You could rely on fear of reprisal for not working to turn in potential spies, but with such difficult living conditions for so many of Chinese laborers, it could be difficult to truly incentivize them through fear of worsening conditions alone.

So the Communist Party in China chose to use a decidedly capitalist approach to the problem of foreign spying: on Monday they announced cash rewards totaling to more than $72,000 (a half million yuan) for information that leads to the apprehension of foreign intelligence actors operating within China.[55]

Better still: they made a cartoon to help teach you how.

The reward system is new, but their public effort to weed out foreign spies isn't. Two years ago, China launched a hotline for citizens to report suspicious foreigners to, and last year as a part of their one year anniversary, they even released a comic-book style poster intended to warn young, female government employees about the dangers of dating "handsome foreigners."

The Beijing Daily Newspaper reported on China's new policy as a mandatory consequence of China's opening up to foreign entities – painting the picture of a direct threat posed by foreigners within China:

"Foreign intelligence organs and other hostile forces have also seized the opportunity to sabotage our country through political infiltration, division and subversion, stealing secrets and collusion," the newspaper said.

Many are concerned, however, that China's new policy, which offers awards ranging from $1,500 – $72,000 for reporting suspicious foreigners, will make serving as a foreign journalist in China more dangerous.

"This is absolutely inexplicable and absurd," Li Fan, founder of the private think tank World and China Institute said. "I don't know what the government is thinking about."

"How can foreign media report here?" he asked. "If you take a photo on the street, somebody will report you as a hostile foreign spy. People will be more cautious to talk to foreign media."[56]

Li, as well as other opponents of new anti-espionage measures have drawn parallels between the financial incentive to turn suspicious people in to the government and the Chinese Cultural Revolution that saw the government encouraging husbands, wives, and even children to turn one another in or denounce their own families in favor of the government.

Of course, China is not the only nation that offers cash rewards for information that benefits investigations into domestic or international threats – and one could argue similar policies in the United States haven't produced a witch-hunt culture, though it bears noting that the United States does not employ a generic cash payout policy for reporting suspicious foreigners.

In the announcement, the Chinese government cited a story from January in which a group of fishermen were rewarded for turning in an "unidentifiable object inscribed with foreign words" they found while trawling for fish. It turned out to be "a spying device that was collecting data on China."[57] What the device was or what nation they claim it originated from was not released, but Chinese officials claimed that there could be additional cash incentives for discoveries that include foreign equipment.

China releases propaganda poster to celebrate its navy, accidentally includes US and Russian military hardware

Last month, China was gearing up to celebrate the 68th anniversary of the establishment of the People's Liberation Army's Navy, which would be punctuated by the launch of the first-ever entirely Chinese-constructed aircraft carrier. On April 23rd, the PLA uploaded a poster to their various social media outlets depicting China's first (and only) aircraft carrier in service, the Liaoning, as well as a few other interesting bits of military gear intended to encourage an outpouring of patriotic support from the Chinese citizenry.[58] However, because of some poorly chosen additions to the image, things didn't turn out quite like they'd hoped.

The poster does indeed depict the Liaoning at sea, a point of pride for the PLA Navy. However, that's about the only thing it gets right. The three fighter jets shown flying above the carrier aren't a part of the PLA, but are rather J-10 "Vigorous Dragon" fighters—a modern jet in Chinese service, but employed only by the PLA Air Force, not the Navy, nor do they have the capability to take off or land on carriers like the one depicted below them.

The problems with the poster only compound from there. The fighter depicted taking off from the deck of the Liaoning isn't Chinese at all, but rather a Russian MiG-35. The MiG-35 is an updated version of the MiG-29 that *does* see use in the Russian military, but not China's. In the distance, behind China's sole aircraft carrier, other naval warships can be seen, but upon closer inspection, it's pretty easy to tell that they also don't hail from the Chinese military.

In fact, the two ships sailing alongside China's pride and joy are actually *San Antonio-class amphibious assault ships* currently in service with *the U.S. Navy*. It can be assumed the PLA's photo/editorial team had intended to use the Kulun Shan-class amphibious ships employed by China's Navy, but based on China's proclivity for stealing other nations' military technology, maybe they just figured no one would notice.[59]

中国海军·拥抱深蓝
68岁生日快乐！
1949-2017
@国防部发布

China's Ministry of National Defense promptly responded to criticism levied both internally and in the international community by issuing a rare formal apology and acknowledging their mistake.[60]

"We have noticed too that the picture wasn't correct and that caused criticism. Our editors made the error but their superiors also share the responsibility," Senior Colonel Yang Yujun, a spokesman for the ministry, told reporters during a scheduled press briefing.

"We believe that the harsh criticisms [from Chinese citizens] reflected their deep love and heartfelt support to us," said Yang. "Leaving the picture along with the appended comments was an alert for us. It serves as a constant reminder to us about working hard and to keep progressing. On behalf of our editing team, we offer our sincere apology as well as gratitude to people who pay attention to us, care about us, and support us."

The government's apology seems to have been well received within the nation, with many Chinese citizens changing their tune in the comments below the picture on various social media platforms to a less critical acknowledgement of their efforts, though the black eye this bit of PR gave the Chinese Navy likely reduced the positive attention the Chinese government have hoped to garner with the official launch of their new carrier.

Image courtesy of the Chinese Ministry of Defense

Jackie Chan tempers anti-U.S. rhetoric long enough to sell you tickets to his new movie

The trailer for the new Jackie Chan/Pierce Brosnan action flick, "The Foreigner," dropped around the world on Monday, and one wouldn't be blamed for thinking this may mark the reemergence of the man who once heralded so much attention in American theaters with action-packed romps like "Rumble in the Bronx." Chan has become a legend in Hollywood for his dangerous stunt work, though he's been absent from America's summer blockbuster industry for a number of years now. The old adage, "absence makes the heart grow fonder," may not be accurate in Chan's case, however, as he's stayed rather busy in his home country of China.

Busy doing what, you ask? Well, making movies of course. Oh, and disparaging America in the media, becoming an outspoken member of the Communist party in China, and even suggesting that Chinese citizens have "too much freedom."[61]

When asked about the United States of America in 2013, Chan called it "The most corrupt in the world," while criticizing Chinese citizens for voicing complaints about their own national government in the press.

"Where does this Great Breakdown [financial crisis] come from? It started exactly from the world, the United States. When I was interviewed in the U.S., people asked me, I said the same thing. I said now that China has become strong, everyone is making an issue of China."[62]

Chan can't be blamed for harboring a patriotic sense of duty to his own nation, but it does seem surprising that he'd go on the offensive regarding the U.S., whose film industry made him an international super star. However, despite Chan's willingness to throw America under the bus, his political leanings haven't won him a great deal of support from the Chinese public either.

In December of 2013, Chan was heavily criticized by many Chinese citizens, particularly citizens of the semi-independent Hong Kong, on social media sites after he suggested China introduce legislation limiting the rights of citizens to protest, as he was distressed that the Chinese people are allowed to "scold China, scold the leaders, scold anything, and protest against anything."

"There should be regulations on what can and cannot be protested," Chan said.[63]

This wasn't the first time Chan spoke out in support of anti-democratic laws, or for Beijing. In 2009, Chan told the Boao Forum for Asia that the Chinese people "need to be controlled."

"I'm not sure if it's good to have freedom or not," Chan said to the crowd. "I'm really confused now. If you're too free, you're like the way Hong Kong is now. It's very chaotic. Taiwan is also chaotic."

"I'm gradually beginning to feel that we Chinese need to be controlled. If we're not being controlled, we'll just do what we want."[64]

Chan's support for Beijing may not be winning him a lot of love on Chinese social media, but it's garnered him a fair amount of support from the Chinese government. They made Chan a national-level delegate of the Chinese People's Political Consultative Conference in 2013, one of the country's most prominent political advisory bodies. While Chan's appointment doesn't provide him with the ability to directly vote on legislation, it serves as a form of official seal of approval on Chan and his work from the Chinese government.

Although tempering his anti-U.S. rhetoric in public appearances since, Chan celebrated the initial success of his movie, "Warcraft" last year by announcing to a crowd of mostly Chinese viewers that it may mark a transition away from the popularity of American movies around the world.

"Warcraft made 600 million RMB [$91 million] in two days — this has scared the Americans," Chan said. "If we can make a film that earns 10 billion [$1.5 billion], then people from all over the world who study film will learn Chinese, instead of us learning English," he added.[65]

Chan's movie "Kung Fu Yoga" that was released early in 2017 also drew criticism for its use of an Indian character shown repeatedly praising President Xi Jinping's Belt and Road Initiative (BRI), which is a Chinese led "connectivity project" the Indian government has thus far declined to join. The movie, which was released in India as well as China, has been called "brazen political propaganda" by critics in both states.[66]

"Kung Fu Yoga" was so heavily laden with pro-Chinese propaganda that Maggie Lee, chief Asia film critic for Variety magazine, wondered if the movie could have survived in its current form if Indian investors originally tied to the film hadn't pulled out.

"However, co-producer Viacom 18, one of Bollywood's biggest studios, soon pulled out. If the partnership had worked, one wonders if Tong [the film's director] would still get away with Chan's character preaching incessantly to Indians about their history to the point where the villain yells, 'Stop teaching me about my own country!' Or such brazen promotion of China's political agenda as having the Indian protagonist exonerate the One Road, One Belt policy," she wrote in her review.

All of this begs the question: is Chan's presence in this new Hollywood movie another attempt at marketing Chinese propaganda to foreign audiences? Well, the trailer certainly seems like there's the potential for it.

In the trailer, Jackie Chan plays a highly trained Chinese operative turned London Chinatown restaurateur who loses his daughter in an IRA bombing. Chan's character then takes on Brosnan, who plays a corrupt British government official, for his involvement in the attack.

Without seeing the film, the plot allots significant opportunity for Chan to play the role of Chinese patriot facing off with Western corruption. The book the movie is based on is, after all, called "The Chinaman."

The trailer goes on to show Chan bombing a government building and setting assorted traps for the British official and his men, accompanied by the tagline, "Never push a good man too far."

Now, it is important to note that lots of great action movies are based on the premise of a corrupt government official (or body) targeting an innocent individual or trying to keep their nefarious deeds under wraps – that in itself isn't what's troubling about Chan's presence in this new film, but rather it's how closely that plot seems to echo Chan's own sentiments about the West that warrants concern. As a man who's faced repeated criticism for using his movies as a mouthpiece for Chinese interests, depicting a "good man" that's forced to take on Western governments because of their corruption makes it hard to ignore his own statements regarding the "corruption" of the United States.

To be fair, this movie could be a great action ride, and may even be entirely on the level when it comes to its representation of the governments and nations depicted within it... but even if it is, do you want your money to go toward funding a resurgence in Chan's American career?

Should people who live in the country Chan refers to as "the most corrupt" in the world go see a movie starring a man that uses his notoriety to claim that he's "not sure if it's good to have freedom?"

Sure, plenty of Americans in Hollywood have ridiculous political beliefs too, but few (if not none) of them also hold an appointed office within the Chinese government, nor have they demonstrated such a proclivity for incorporating those politics into their work in a manner intended to benefit a foreign government.

For my money, I'll just re-watch an old DVD copy of Rush Hour, and skip this one. Thanks anyway.

China begins accompanying Hollywood blockbusters with propaganda films in theaters

China's military is amidst a period of expansion and reorganization, which has drawn quite a bit of attention in areas like the South China Sea, but less focus has been placed on China's growing propaganda efforts, particularly in the realm of cinema.

China has rapidly become the second, or arguably even the first, most important market for movie executives clamoring to launch the next multi-billion-dollar franchise. The Chinese market can account for hundreds of millions of dollars per movie, even saving films that would have once been considered bombs for failing to court a substantial U.S. box office gross.[67] Movies like Michael Bay's "Transformers" series have the Asian market to thank for their large returns, and Blizzard's "Warcraft" was not only saved by a big Chinese opening, it prompted Jackie Chan to predict the end of America's grip on the blockbuster market.

However, unlike in the United States, China's government exerts a great deal of control over the media it permits in its theaters. This influence has resulted in dramatic changes to movies produced here in the United States. The 2012 remake of "Red Dawn" depicted the Chinese as America's invaders, but they were forced to go back and change all of the flags to North Korean ones in post-production when China declared they wouldn't allow its release. Adam Sandler's disappointment, "Pixels," was also forced to remove a scene that showed the destruction of the Great Wall of China, and Marvel's

"Doctor Strange" had to change the nationality of "the ancient one" to avoid making any mention of Tibet, again, in order to secure China's approval.

This propaganda effort seeks returns from two distinct markets: China hopes to manage perceptions of itself in foreign markets, while also shifting beliefs within their own borders. Movies like last year's "Kung Fu Yoga" have been accused of overtly inserting propaganda aimed at Indian audiences regarding China's Belt and Road Initiative (BRI) connectivity project, but even simply exerting control and influence over the content depicted in films seems to fall short of accomplishing China's larger propaganda goals, so now, all movies shown in China will be accompanied by brief films of their favorite actors and actresses singing the praises of China's government.

Thus far, four films, dubbed "The Glory and the Dream — Our Chinese Dream," began airing before all movies on July 1st. These propaganda films, dubbed "PSAs" by authorities "are aimed at helping the public better understand and accept the policies and visions of the Party," explains the State Administration of Press, Publication, Radio, Film and Television, which championed the new project.

The titles of these first four short films are the "Chinese Dream," the "Core Values of Socialism," the "Four Comprehensives," and the "Five-in-one Overall Arrangement."

"Beijing seems determined to exercise ever greater control, injecting itself even into entertainment," said Kevin Carrico, a lecturer of Chinese studies in Macquarie University. "This grows out of the very simplistic and antiquarian nature of Beijing's propaganda [and] media system in contrast to the complexity of contemporary Chinese society."[68]

A number of Chinese celebrities are signed on to create these films, all at no charge, though the most prominent name in the group may be familiar to some of SOFREP's subscribers: Jackie Chan.

"Only when the country and the nation fare well, will everybody fare well," a smiling Chan says to the camera in front of a grey backdrop. "Only when everyone fights for a beautiful dream, can they come together with the tremendous power to realize the Chinese dream," he continues.

Of course, whether or not such an overt attempt at shaping opinion can be successful in the modern world of media saturation is far from certain. This form of propaganda had its heyday in World War II, but the media climate and average viewer's manipulation literacy is far different today.

"There is some degree of sophistication to this latest propaganda salvo," says Willy Lam, a longtime China observer at the Chinese University of Hong Kong. "The fact that the Chinese dream-related slogans are spoken by well-known movie and cultural personalities might attract the attention of a part of the audience."

However, Lam remains unconvinced that this project will work out for China the way they hope.

"Most Chinese, especially young people, are very fed up with in-your-face state propaganda. It's doubtful whether cinema-goers will actually pay any attention to the slogans."

By Alex Hollings

New Chinese propaganda game goes viral: Measures who can clap fastest for President Xi Jinping

A great deal of attention has been paid to outwardly directed influence campaigns mounted by world governments in recent months. At the forefront of the public's attention has been Russia, due to their efforts to influence voters leading up to the 2016 Presidential election and following efforts to sow discord within the American people in places like Charlottesville, where some Americans were more than happy to sow some discord of their own. Throughout all the posturing, bravado and tap dancing exhibited on both sides of the aisle regarding Russian influence, however, little attention has been paid to another nation that produces propaganda at a varsity level: China.

We've already addressed China's massive and ever-growing influence on American motion pictures. Huge investments from China have injected Chinese interests into a number of major studios, and the government's formal censorship practices demand that no content that can be construed as even remotely anti-Chinese makes it onto the screen, or else the movie will be banned from the second largest paying audience in the world. We've also already discussed their internal propaganda efforts, employing big names like Jackie Chan to force influence into popular culture wherever they feel able. Many of these efforts, however, have proven less than effective, as modern culture and technology intertwine into an amalgam of non-stop exposure and market saturation-induced cynicism.

China's most recent effort, however, may have cracked the code when it comes to appealing to the younger generation of citizens that have proven extremely difficult to influence by traditional means; a smart phone applications. More specifically, it's a game.

How do you play? Simple really. You just watch Chinese President Xi Jinping deliver a speech that, among other things, stresses the benefits of "socialism with Chinese characteristics" and then you see how much you can *clap*.

That's it. You just try to clap for President Xi's speech faster and harder than your friends. If that sounds silly, you probably aren't one of the people with Candy Crush open in another window.

Called "Excellent Speech: Clap for Xi Jinping," the new game brought to the Chinese public by the same tech giant that produces popular games like "League of Legends," the game has already been played more than *400 million times* since its release on Wednesday.[69] Game play entails watching snippets of Xi's speech, followed by tapping the screen to clap your digital hands as quickly as possible for 19 second intervals. Once the game is over, you're shown your results, as well as where you stack up against other clappers.

Ironically, a number of political figures within China were seen yawning or dozing off during the three-and-a-half-hour speech this game derives its content from. Apparently, the speech is much more dynamic as an app, as one user bragged about clapping some "1,695 times" during a single play through. By 3 pm on Thursday, the total number of "claps" recorded by the game, according to its landing page, was over a billion.

Whether or not this digital craze will result in a palpable shift in the way young Chinese citizens see their government is yet to be seen, but its success will undoubtedly ensure that this won't be the last time the

Chinese people are encouraged to listen to, and then "clap" for their president's talking points.

By Alex Hollings

NORTH KOREAN EFFORTS

By Alex Hollings

North Korean national celebration culminates with video of ICBM strike on the United States

North Korea has become a common topic of conversation in the United States lately, as many fear their missile program and unwillingness to negotiate with the international community may result in a military standoff that could potentially turn nuclear. America has been at the forefront of this issue, but many other nations have voiced their support. Even North Korea's primary ally, China, has begun to make nice with President Trump to a certain extent; acknowledging that even they must play a role in limiting Kim Jong Un's access to weapons of mass destruction.

Here in the States, we argue and debate about the missile strike in Syria, the MOAB in Afghanistan, and the potential for war with North Korea. Our politicians hash it out on national television, our president makes statements about seeking a diplomatic solution if at all possible, and our media and culture tends to paint taking military action as a negative thing – our society values human life, and in particular, the lives of innocent civilians. Since Vietnam, we as people have romanticized real warfare less, as we've come to understand that war is often inextricably tied to the suffering of the innocent, and as such, should be considered the last option to be employed.

North Korea, on the other hand, doesn't benefit from the public discussion of differing viewpoints, or the freedom of a press that shows us the reality of war. The people in the reclusive Asian nation are permitted to consume only media distributed through state-owned outlets, and because the Kim dynasty does not require elections, there are no political debates to witness.

This aligns North Korea as an interesting sociological experiment. While we may attempt to study the media choices employed by totalitarian regimes of the past like Adolf Hitler and the Nazi party, North Korea allows us to see, in real-time, what a despot will do to manage the perceptions of his people. One such opportunity came last weekend, as North Korea celebrated the birth of Kim Il Sung, the current leader's grandfather, and the founder of their republic. Kim Il Sung is such an important figure in North Korea, they restarted their calendar to reflect his birth as the very beginning of time – meaning it is not the year 2017 in North Korea, but rather the year 105; a fact displayed by the military aircraft flying above their parade in the form of those very numbers.

While American Fourth of July celebrations often end with fireworks, North Korea opted for something a bit different. Kim Jong Un watched as an orchestra played over a brief video that opened with patriotic images like we might see in our own celebrations, but closed with a scene depicting a North Korean missile strike on a coastal American city. The explosion gives way to a view of a burning American flag waving above the white crosses at Arlington National Cemetery.[70]

Outside of North Korea, watching their day of celebration culminate in a fictitious depiction of murdering thousands, or millions, of innocent people seems a bit... harsh, but for North Koreans that are raised to believe their strife is the product of a world led by the United States and bent on their destruction, it likely seems almost ordinary.

By Alex Hollings

Dennis Rodman's new trip to North Korea is reminder that dictators use celebrities for marketing too

Dennis Rodman is a name we all somehow still remember, despite his contributions to basketball, film, and international politics all ranging from forgettable to... well... unforgivable. The man who once played alongside Michael Jordan while making public appearances in a wedding dress would eventually go on to star in terrible movies alongside Jean Claude Van Dam, before ultimately grasping for the last bit of headline-worthy stardom he could reach, and serving alongside a dictator as the tallest cog in the North Korean propaganda machine.

We've been blessed by a reprieve of Rodman's antics in recent years, but all good things must come to an end, and he now believes that another trip to the reclusive North Korean state is in order amid serious tensions surrounding his friend, Kim Jong Un, and the dictator's relentless pursuit of nuclear weapons.

You may think calling the cruel dictator, Kim Jong Un, Rodman's "friend" is a form of editorializing, but it's actually how Rodman himself refers to him. Rodman is also quick to point out that Kim is a "very good guy."

Ya know, aside from all the estimated hundred thousand Korean citizens he has in labor camps thanks to a policy of punishing three generations of a family for crimes committed by an individual, the regular propaganda he has released showing North Korea destroying American cities with nuclear weapons, ordering the assassination of his own half-brother, and that sort of stuff.[71] Dennis Rodman probably means *aside* from that sort of stuff.

When asked if Rodman planned to use any of his facetime with the Korean dictator to address the four Americans that are still being detained by the North Korean government, Rodman seemed as disinterested in their plight as he is about the North Korean people living under Kim's rule.

"Well that's not my purpose right now... My purpose is to go over there and try to see if I can keep bringing sports to North Korea," he told CNN. In his defense, North Korea could probably use some help bolstering their professional sports. A lack of food can really hinder an athlete's ability to perform.

In fairness to Rodman, some believe he sees his trips as an act of goodwill intended to help warm over relations between North Korea and the United States.[72]

"We all have specialties, but Dennis does have a view about human beings and the natural state of affairs — his view seems to me is that if people will talk and interact and if there's dialogue and exchanges and interactions, this process will naturally lead to de-escalation," explained Daniel Pinkston, a professor of International Relations at Troy University in Seoul.

Rodman seems to either think that his efforts may actually help, or at least that he can convince some Stateside that his trips are about something bigger than his own dying celebrity status. Although Rodman ignored questions about whether or not he would be meeting with Kim directly during his visit as he was mobbed by press at the Beijing airport, he did respond when asked if he'd spoken to President Trump about the visit. Rodman appeared on Trump's reality show "Celebrity Apprentice" twice, and endorsed him for president.

"I'm pretty sure he's happy at the fact that I'm over here trying to accomplish something that we both need." Rodman said of the American president. Of course, he also made sure to show off his tee-shirt that advertises the marijuana based digital currency that's sponsoring him... because Rodman cares about bringing basketball to the masses only slightly more than he cares about securing a ridiculous endorsement deal.

Rodman, it would seem, has fallen into the same trap that brought Limp Bizkit front man Fred Durst to Crimea where he set about producing Russian propaganda films backed by the Kremlin. Is it because these celebrities are too foolish to appreciate that they're simply tools being used to shape public perception? That seems likely. Guys like Durst and Rodman see their fame fading in the United States, but these oppressive regimes, eager to find a face they can stick in front of cameras as an indicator that maybe they're "not so bad after all," are happy to play the part of star-struck fans – injecting a sense of importance into the deflating self-esteem of celebrities like them with a desperate need for the spotlight.

Should we care that Dennis Rodman is heading back into North Korea? That depends. It seems incredibly unlikely that his presence will have any effect on U.S./North Korean relations, nor does it seem as though Rodman himself is interested in helping advance U.S. strategy in the region.

The only thing we really need to be cognizant of is how Rodman tries to present Kim's North Korean regime upon his return. Like Tom Cruise and Scientology, Kim knows Rodman will have an audience, and he will almost certainly work to manipulate Rodman into believing – and sharing his belief – that Kim is the victim of American hostility; which has been the North Korean PR strategy for months now.

The only damage Rodman can do at this point is work to change our cultural perception of Kim and his despotic rule – something we can all expect out of the interviews he has almost certainly already started booking for his return.

Did North Korea just admit Kim's been lying about their nukes?

Kim Jong un's North Korean regime are no strangers to exaggeration when it comes to threats levied toward the United States and its allies. In fact, up until recently, there were really only two things you could count on in terms of North Korean diplomacy: that they would offer up outlandish threats, and that the majority of the rest of the world would chuckle, offer them the geopolitical equivalent of a pat on the head, and get back to more pressing matters.

Over the past year or so, however, things have changed. Six nuclear tests, including one that appeared to be a successful detonation of dual-stage, or hydrogen bomb, in conjunction with a litany of successful and failed ballistic missile tests have proven that Kim is no longer just a little guy with a big mouth – he's suddenly a dangerous dictator with a stockpile of weapons of mass destruction.

Nonetheless, Kim's regime has maintained the status quo in terms of outward communication, continuing to threaten the world at large with colorfully described, violent retribution for each perceived slight, to include a number of threats of preemptive nuclear strikes. Tests of the North Korean missile platform called the Hwasong-14 left experts within the United States reeling – as it appeared to demonstrate a flight path that would place cities on America's East Coast within its range, just as they have claimed.

Issues muddied the water, however, including the apparent failure of the reentry vehicle on the platform, suggesting North Korea still has some work to do before effectively delivering a warhead, and a number of experts believed the dummy warhead affixed to the missile was actually significantly lighter than a real nuclear weapon would be, allowing it to demonstrate a flight capability that it couldn't match in a real launch.

Nonetheless, the Hwasong-14 appeared to be, at least potentially, capable of striking nearly any target within the continental United States, which when paired with their recent development of thermonuclear warheads, made for a pretty troubling revelation. Kim, eager to capitalize on that revelation, issued a series of new threats, claiming that the entire United States mainland was now within his nuclear strike capability in public statements dating back at least as far as June of this year.

Now though, North Korea seems willing to admit that they don't currently possess the capability they've been touting for months, as one North Korean official told CNN this week that the nation's Supreme Leader won't be willing to turn to diplomacy until North Korea possesses the ability to strike "all the way to the East coast of the mainland U.S."

"Before we can engage in diplomacy with the Trump administration, we want to send a clear message that the DPRK has a reliable defensive and offensive capability to counter any aggression from the United States," the official said, according to CNN.[73]

That means, in no uncertain terms, that they currently don't have a reliable platform that could ferry their warheads across the globe. That does, of course, contradict Kim's statement in June, saying, "the entire U.S. mainland" is in reach, or the official government statement released through KCNA, a state-owned news outlet, in July.[74]

"We have demonstrated our ability to fire our intercontinental ballistic rocket at any time and place and that the entire U.S. territory is within our shooting range," the statement ran, citing Kim himself.[75]

Ultimately, all this proves is something we already knew – that North Korean statements aren't to be trusted, but it is unusual for state officials to contradict a statement made by Kim, especially one made so often and recently. It also suggests that more long range ballistic missile tests will be forthcoming, as it's more clear now than ever that Kim sees nuclear tipped ICBMs as a shortcut to being taken seriously at the negotiating table – and if he doesn't have them now, you can be sure he'll continue to push for them to the dismay of the international community, and the suffering of his own people, until he does.

By Alex Hollings

North Korea may soon have the ability to follow through on decades of threats, but U.S. resolve is wavering

In recent months, North Korea's despotic Supreme Leader, Kim Jong Un, has continued his pursuit of nuclear weapons, and ballistic missile platforms capable of delivering them to targets all around the globe, but a distinct shift in rhetoric coming from the region has begun to alter our American perspective of the situation. In the minds of many, heightened tensions with North Korea could be attributed to America's controversial and conservative president, because those who disagree with Donald Trump would rather attribute all of the problems this country faces to his spray tan, rather than approach each with an objective and analytical mindset.

The thing is, North Korea has been an issue since well before Trump took office, and the situation we find ourselves in now is nothing more than the natural escalation of Kim's rule. The only elements of this scenario that have really changed during the Trump presidency are how close Kim finally is to achieving his goal, and how much attention we're paying to the situation in the media.

Recognizing that they stand little chance of winning a staring contest with multiple carrier strike groups and nearly 30,000 American soldiers bolstering South Korean defenses just south of the demilitarized zone, North Korea decided to follow Vladimir Putin's lead a few months ago and start working to take charge of the narrative. Instead of working tirelessly to present the image of a military peer worthy of fear and respect (as they have so comically attempted in the past), North Korea is now trying to paint a very different picture: one where they admit to being smaller and less powerful – in order to pretend they're the victim of geopolitical bullying, rather than being subject to the same rule of law that governs most modern nations.

In short, North Korea is pointing its well-honed propaganda machine outward for a change, and it's beginning to work. Kim, or at least his advisors, seem well aware that they don't need to *win* a fight on their shores to defeat America, they just need to alter how the American people see a conflict with them. A strategic military victory in the Pacific could even bolster American support for war with North Korea... but if there's one thing modern American culture truly hates, it's a bully. By making it seem like our government is that bully, North Korea, as well as other competitors like Russia, can begin to deflate American support for a war before it ever develops.

So let's take this opportunity to look back on some of North Korea's statements to the world at large before they started pretending they're the victim of a Trump-led conspiracy intent on ruining their chances at financial security (by way of strong arming trade deals through nuclear threats, as Kim hopes to do).

In 2009, North Korea's government issued a statement to announce that it had "tremendous military muscle and its own method of strike able to conquer any targets in its vicinity at one stroke or hit the U.S. on the raw, if necessary."[76]

In 2013, the North Korean government released images of Kim and his top military advisors pouring over documents with a map in the background that read, "US Mainland Strike Plan."[77] The image was accompanied in state-owned media outlets with the description: "He finally signed the plan on technical preparations of strategic rockets, ordering them to be on standby to fire so that they may strike any time the U.S. mainland, its military bases in the operational theaters in the Pacific, including Hawaii and Guam, and those in south Korea," a KCNA report in English said.

Another statement in 2013 read, "Now that the US is set to light a fuse for a nuclear war, (our) revolutionary armed forces... will exercise the right to a pre-emptive nuclear attack to destroy the strongholds of the aggressors."[78]

"The moment of explosion is approaching fast," the statement read, warning that war could break out "today or tomorrow."

In July of 2014, the director of the general political bureau of North Korea's military claimed, "If the U.S. imperialists threaten our sovereignty and survival ... our troops will fire our nuclear-armed rockets at the White House and the Pentagon — the sources of all evil."

In February of 2015, North Korea declared, "Since the gangster-like US imperialists are blaring that they will 'bring down' the DPRK (North Korea) ... the army and people of the DPRK cannot but officially notify the Obama administration ... that the DPRK has neither need nor willingness to sit at negotiating table with the US any longer."

It added that the North was capable of bringing about the "final ruin of the US" with its "precision and diversified nuclear striking means."[79]

Let's be clear, this is neither a complete list, nor is it even a list of their most egregious threats against the United States – it's literally just a collection of the most easily accessible threats North Korea has levied in the past few years. You could devote the rest of your day to finding examples of North Korea threatening pre-emptive nuclear strikes against America and its allies, or the propaganda videos Kim's regime has released depicting the destruction of U.S. cities. The thing is, none of this surprises any of you, because you've heard it all before.

So why are we starting to second guess whether or not North Korea is a dangerous enemy, not only of the United States, but to stability in the Pacific? Is it because our internal political disputes are more important that our own actual physical safety? Or is it because we're so saturated with media content, that we can be easily persuaded to change our minds about things we once knew with certainty?

Maybe they're just that good at PR.

Don't be persuaded by the "everything America does is bad," rhetoric, and don't fall into the "if we just left bad guys alone, they'd stop being bad!" logical trap we hear from our society's great thinkers (like Katy Perry). Instead, look at the evidence, and decide for yourself. It's easy to find a thousand think pieces, podcasts, and essays written about how uncomfortable left-leaning folks are with Donald Trump's finger on the nuclear button...

So we should ask ourselves... shouldn't we be *more* concerned with this guy's nukes instead?

A war with North Korea isn't inevitable, nor is it in our best interest... but we must remain unwavering and resolute about allowing Kim to develop weapons of mass destruction, otherwise we're approaching the diplomatic negotiating table with a weak hand and little hope for success.

By Alex Hollings

North Korea now taking cues from Russia, trying to change the narrative of their standoff with US

Since it's very inception, North Korea's nuclear weapons-development program has primarily been about changing North Korea's footing in the geopolitical theater. Kim Jong-un believes that having an arsenal of nuclear weapons will force states like the U.S. to approach his nation with more peer-like respect, as one of the few nuclear powers on the globe. Kim's hunt for nukes has never been about using them so much as it's been about being able to threaten their use, and to use those threats as leverage to improve trade and political relations between the world and his small nation, whose entire GDP makes up only a fifteenth of what the U.S. spends on defense alone.

And now, thanks to public posturing by Russia and China on North Korea's behalf, they've seemingly adopted a new strategy that runs counter to their repeated threats of nuclear annihilation: playing the victim.

In public statements made over the course of the past few weeks, Russia has portrayed the developing situation on the Korean Peninsula as "international bullying," blaming the United States for inciting the North Koreans with its military presence and accusing the American government of trying to intimidate the small nation.

"We need to act in a joined-up way, (and) strengthen the system of international guarantees with the help of international law and with the help of the U.N. Charter," Putin said last week. "We need to return to dialogue with North Korea and stop scaring it and find ways to resolve these problems peacefully."[80]

"The combative rhetoric coupled with reckless muscle-flexing has led to a situation where the whole world seriously is now wondering whether there's going to be a war or not," Russian Deputy Foreign Minister Gennady Gatilov told the U.N. Security Council earlier this month. "One ill-thought-out or misinterpreted step could lead to the most frightening and lamentable consequences."

This depiction of the U.S. roughing up the little guy doesn't seem to logically follow the rhetoric coming from within Kim's regime: things like showing videos of North Korean nukes obliterating American cities during their equivalent of a 4th of July parade, or issuing repeated threats of conducting pre-emptive nuclear strikes on U.S. bases on allied land in South Korea and Japan. From every objective viewpoint, North Korea's posturing has been aggressive and often unwarranted. While other nations interact through veiled threats amid polite conversation, North Korea has long skipped that political courtesy and defaulted to exclaiming that they'll wipe America's "evil empire" off the map.

That is, until this week, during which North Korea sent letters of protest to the U.S. Congress and other nations enacting further sanctions on the aggressive state, referring to the sanctions as a "heinous act against humanity" and arguing in favor of loosening restrictions on trade. Couple this with North Korea's recent unsubstantiated accusations that the CIA and South Korean Intelligence Service conspired with a former North Korean lumberjack to assassinate their supreme leader, and a PR strategy begins to emerge.[81] North Korea is no longer trying to depict themselves as a military competitor with the U.S., it now hopes to illicit international support through sympathy—or pity. It's unlikely they'd care which.

"As everybody knows, the Americans have gestured (toward) dialogue," North Korea's Deputy U.N. Ambassador Kim In Ryong told reporters on Friday. "But what is important is not words, but actions.

The rolling back of the hostile policy toward DPRK is the prerequisite for solving all the problems in the Korean Peninsula. Therefore, the urgent issue to be settled on Korean Peninsula is to put a definite end to the U.S. hostile policy toward DPRK, the root cause of all problems."

The root cause of all problems. That's an important sentence to note.

North Korea's new statements are part of a concerted effort to change the narrative on the Korean Peninsula, and as silly as that may seem, it's entirely possible that they will. The Russian media machine is churning out headlines that paint Americans as transgressors that illegally overstep their bounds in Syria and North Korea. They've even begun using the same perception management techniques put to use in the 2016 presidential election, and North Korea seems to be aware of that.

Combined with the anti-Trump sentiment held throughout much of the European Union's leadership, concerns about the future of NATO, and an ongoing investigation into President Trump's staff potentially colluding with the Russians in order to get into office, and you have the recipe for a world population that could potentially be ready to change sides on this subject, as the narrative continues to point toward this being about American aggression rather than North Korean.

It's impossible to know whether or not Russia intended for Kim's regime to get on board with their list of talking points, but it has become clear that Putin is seeking warmer relations with the isolated country.[82]

China, though publicly supporting a denuclearized Korean Peninsula, has also made repeated statements indicating that the U.S. shares fault for the current predicament. China is admittedly a strained ally of Kim's government, but their relations remain significantly warmer that those maintained between China and the U.S.

Ultimately, the loudest voices out of the Pacific will continue to be China's and Russia's, neither of which would benefit from a conclusion to the North Korean standoff that sees the United States and its allies taking military action. Logically, they'd be invested in keeping the peace, and in hurting U.S. foreign interests in the region however they could.

That isn't to say that military action is the necessary or only potential outcome of this scenario, but the threat of it has given North Korea and some nations friendly to their cause the ammunition they need to launch a preemptive PR campaign, rather than a military one.

The question is, will the people of the world buy it?

By Alex Hollings

AMERICAN EFFORTS

By Alex Hollings

Op-Ed: Russia's paying to post lies in your newsfeed... but do we have the moral high ground?

The recent revelation that Russian entities funneled money into marketing on social media platforms like Facebook in order to create dissent within the American population, particularly regarding the 2016 presidential election, has made waves on social media, and for good reason.[83] With many Americans continuing to counter concerns about Russian meddling as either non-existent or inconsequential, the discovery that foreign interests are willing to invest millions of dollars into influencing internal American politics should serve as an indicator that these practices are not only effective, but commonplace.

For those within America's intelligence community, this wasn't a revelation at all. We've been well aware of how successful these kinds of operations can be for decades. After all, we've done our fair share of them ourselves.

The thing about international diplomacy is that it has always required a "do as I say, not as I do" mindset, especially when it comes to intelligence operations. Every once in a while, a story will break about a Chinese spy stealing plans for a defense project, and we as a nation gasp as their audacity – while American intelligence agents operating all over the world shrug and wonder if it was poor trade craft or a leak that got that guy burned... hoping the same doesn't happen to them. The common axiom, "all's fair in love and war," isn't exactly right – it's more like "all's fair in international intel and psy-ops -- as long as you don't get caught."

The United States has been complicit in a number of high and low profile regime changes over the years, and throughout, we've justified those actions by using cause and effect rationale to paint a picture of justification in the interest of our own security. That isn't anti-American sentiments creeping past my patriotic seeming exterior, it's an honest and objective assessment of America's foreign policy. It isn't that we're *bad guys*, it's that, when it comes to global conflict, there are no good guys and bad guys, there can only be "us" and "them." No matter how elevated you may feel on your moral high ground, it doesn't actually offer a superior firing position.

Sometimes, in the interest of national security, the American government (often as a compartmentalized portion rather than as a whole) chooses to cross the lines we've drawn in the sand as a basis for our own moral superiority. Sometimes these are military operations, sometimes they're propaganda campaigns, and chances are, sometimes they exist within the digital sphere... just like Russia's. Again, it's important to recognize that, as Americans, we see many of our own violations of international decency as a necessary ugliness, in the interest of continued American prosperity. It is, however, equally important that we appreciate that same mindset is permeating throughout the Russian government as well.

As Mikhail Gorbachev, the last leader of the Soviet Union, came to power in 1985, he brought with him ideas of loosening government restrictions on individual rights (an important tenet of Glasnost) and incorporating elements of capitalism into the Russian economy intended to steer it toward a more functional model like that currently employed by China. These reforms, which would ultimately lead to the end of the Soviet Union, were not just casually observed from American shores, they were ushered along by a concerted public effort, coupled with a number of undercover campaigns, initiated by Jimmy Carter and later further emboldened by President Ronald Reagan, who ran on a platform that included a strong current of anti-Soviet rhetoric.

Reagan, in particular, delivered an influx of military spending, which led to new and improved weapons platforms, capabilities, and defensive strategies. In effect, Reagan, for the first time since the start of the Cold War, saw the first significant leap ahead of Soviet military capabilities, including in America's missile defense strategies, which meant the long-standing tradition of "mutually assured destruction" was no longer quite as assured on the American side. These advancements, coupled with a policy of Soviet economic isolation championed by the United States, led the, now far more liberated, Soviet citizenry to become extremely critical of their government.

Outside the public eye, the CIA began probing Russian defenses using aircraft that flew unannounced routes over the North Pole toward the Soviet Union or that penetrated protected airspace briefly near Asia. These flights were not recorded in any files to maintain secrecy, according to CIA documents that have since been released, and were not intended to convey any actual intentions to the Soviets.[84] These flights, which commenced in the early days of Reagan's administration, were for no purpose other than to unnerve Soviet defense officials as America began to take the lead in military capability. Aircraft weren't the only ones playing this game either.

According to published accounts, the U.S. Navy played a key role in the PSYOP program after President Reagan authorized it in March 1981 to operate and exercise near maritime approaches to the USSR, in places where U.S. warships "had never gone before," the CIA states. "These exercises reportedly included secret operations that simulated surprise naval air attacks on Soviet targets."

These behaviors, some of which seem to closely parallel recent Russian behavior around the world, were only a part of a massive coordinated effort to go to war with the Russian *ideology*, because actual combat operations would have been too costly, in terms of dollars and human life, to conduct. Now, as Russia works to regain its foothold as a global power, it has continued in the Cold War tradition of matching public posturing with underhanded efforts to destabilize and weaken its opponent. From our perspective, that makes them bad guys, but objectively, this is simply one facet of war's natural progression.

So what does all this objective historical analysis really mean in the scope of today's challenges? Certainly not that we should permit Russia to continue to work to influence American's perceptions of their own country, president, or government. Embracing a foreign nation's psychological campaigns would be paramount to surrender, and even politely ignoring it results in defeat -- just ask Gorbachev. The intent behind this (admittedly broad stroked) jaunt back through American history also isn't meant to point out that America is "just as bad as" anyone else, or to justify another nation's bad behavior by comparing it to America's own. That concept is inherently flawed, because in the grand scope of things, "bad behavior" (in terms of efforts to manipulate foreign politics) is often just a matter of perspective.

Instead, the idea behind drawing a comparison between Russia's recent efforts at election manipulation and our own history of usurping leaders with unfriendly intentions is to show that war is ongoing, even when shots aren't being fired. Russia isn't going to stop trying to meddle in our elections, though they'll likely begin to adjust their methods until they find one that rests quietly below the surface of our collective perception once again. The United States isn't going to stop anytime soon either – because doing so would leave the development of the world just outside our borders to fate, and when it comes to the wellbeing of hundreds of millions of Americans, to do so would be irresponsible.

What we need to do, as increasingly privy American people, is combat foreign influence campaigns the good old-fashioned way, while America's defensive infrastructure continues to root them out. The intelligence game continues to thrive because the "bad guys" will continue to develop new ways to win, while our "good guys" try to figure those ways out and counter them. Back in World War II, doing your part in the war effort included buying war bonds and building a freedom garden in your yard. Today, it means looking at the crap you see on your Facebook newsfeed with a critical eye, and considering the sources they came from.

Looking back at our collective history objectively and saying, "yeah, we've all played this game," might mean some may have trouble bridging the gap between their perceived American moral high ground when it comes to these types of endeavors and the reality that we're embroiled in continual combat with another global power, though it's one in the communications realm rather than the physical one. Reality has a nasty way of not caring about our moral sensibilities in that regard. Likewise, we can use our understanding of history, and how successful America's psyops campaigns were in places like the Soviet Union, to help us to better understand and counter modern foreign efforts to do the same to us.

We, as a people, may have a habit of pointing at the man in the White House, or the thousands of Americans tasked with protecting us from foreign influence as those at fault, but the real soldiers on the front lines of this fight... are us. Russian propaganda being marketed through social media only works as long we click, read, share, and *believe* the messages they're sending.

Russia produces content, and pays to market it on social media – like they're producing bullets for a gun. They're paying up front to get the bullets to us, but that doesn't force us to shoot them at our friends. You decide what you share. You decide what sources you trust. You can win this fight for all of us.

Air Force testing leaflet cluster bombs that could be used to communicate with North Korea's isolated populous

The potential for an armed conflict with North Korea has raised some concerns the United States military hasn't been faced with in some time. How well America's missile defenses will work against a nuclear tipped ICBM may be the most prominent among them, but other concerns, such as how America and its allies might communicate with the isolated population of North Korea during a time of war, are also important to devising an overall military strategy in the event that diplomacy fails.

While internet connectivity is prevalent throughout much of the world, and even in many developing nations one might not be surprised to find themselves logging into Facebook; North Korea remains behind a self-imposed communications blackout. By strictly limiting access to the World Wide Web, Kim Jong Un and his regime are able to maintain control over much of the information that reaches the nation's populous, permitting him the ability to manage the perceptions of the citizenry. The decision to limit internet access within North Korea is only a portion of Kim's overall propaganda strategy, which also includes a mandatory radio in every home with *no off button*, through which the North Korean government can provide all the information a "well informed" North Korean citizen needs to hear, at least as far as Kim is concerned.

If the United States were to go to war with North Korea, it goes without saying that the targets of America's military apparatus would all be military related, but the nature of such a war would mean many of those military related assets would undoubtedly be found in population centers that could produce catastrophic civilian casualties. There was a time when America and its allies might have relied on carpet bombing a nation in order to cripple its economic infrastructure in order to slow or stop the development of weapons, equipment, and ammunition. In modern warfare, however, the American people have grown far less accepting of the carpet bombing methodology, and likely would not tolerate a strategy that leveraged its success on the backs of so many innocent people.

Logically then, the United States would want to get a message to the people of North Korea – perhaps warning them to evacuate an area before bombs or missiles were sent their way, or possibly to counter disinformation being delivered to them by way of their own formal government. With no television, radio, or internet from the outside world reaching the citizens of the Democratic People's Republic of Korea (DPRK, as they refer to themselves), a new method of delivery would have to be employed.

Or maybe just an updated version of an old one, would suffice.

The U.S. Air Force recently began testing a new cluster bomb in the skies over test ranges in California, only instead of delivering ordnance to a target, they're designed to deliver leaflets. The U.S. military has been working to phase out the use of cluster bombs, as they tend to leave unexploded ordnance on the ground where they're used, and have proven to be long-term threats to the population of the area. Instead of simply doing away with these platforms however, the Air Force now hopes to repurpose bombs like the MK. 20 Rockeye II by hollowing them out to carry leaflets instead of explosives.

Two tests were conducted in late July, one over the Point Mugu Sea Test Range and the other over Edwards Air Force Base. The leaflet bombs were dropped from B-52 bombers crewed by the 419th Flight Test Squadron. A total of eight PDU-5/B bombs were dropped in the two tests, each capable of containing some 60,000 leaflets.[85]

Dropping leaflets from aircraft has been a common facet of communicating with enemy troops on the ground, as well as civilians in foreign controlled territory. Leaflet drops occurred in World War II and have continued through to modern operations in Iraq, but the new delivery system the Air Force is testing could potentially cover a far larger territory than previous methods, which may prove valuable if ever America is forced to actively target assets in a heavily populated place... like Pyongyang.

By Alex Hollings

Domestic Perception Management

"In wartime, truth is so precious that she should always be attended by a bodyguard of lies."
— Winston S. Churchill

While the United States has proven reluctant to participate in the same sort of narrative and perception management techniques we've seen employed both internationally and domestically by nations like China, Russia or North Korea, that isn't to say that there has been no effort to skew the ways Americans see their own defense apparatus. Unlike in many other nations, there are laws pertaining to the ways the U.S. Government can engage in direct messaging efforts among its own populous, though adjustments to those laws over the years have shown that the laws themselves are subject to change as the government identifies the shifting needs in its messaging apparatus.

However, America's formal perception management endeavors aimed at the American public are often fairly basic when compared to the efforts put forth not only by foreign governments, but by the two dominant political parties within the nation itself. Nonetheless, these efforts, though not necessarily malign in their intentions, are worthy of discussion and analysis. After all, any time someone is working to sway your perceptions, it pays to be paying close attention.

Marvel's decision to partner with Northrop Grumman is nothing new, but canceling it is

In what will likely be seen as a case study for business and marketing majors in the years to come, Marvel recently announced a joint venture with defense contractor Northrop Grumman, only to quickly cancel their plans to partner with the corporation after receiving a significantly negative response on social media, accusing the comic book company of joining forces with a war profiteer.

This backlash couldn't have come at a more difficult time for the company that has turned into a television and cinema powerhouse, but has seen consistent drops in sales for their namesake comic books.[86] A combination of things can be blamed for Marvel's lost revenue on the printed side of the house: their clunky efforts toward adopting digital distribution methods, their shift toward releasing multiple special edition cover variants of single issues for collectors instead of good stories for readers, or just the gradual shift in the way the American public chooses to spend its time... but Marvel has responded to the lower numbers with a series of controversial decisions that have drawn the ire of groups on both the right and left side of the American political divide.

Heroes and stories have been changed to match what some on the right consider to be "liberal leaning" views, and attempts to grab headlines by doing things like making Captain America a secret Nazi, unsurprisingly to us normal people, didn't result in a huge influx of sales past the initial issue that first drew the world's attention.

Which brings us to their latest scandal – the short-lived partnership of Marvel Comics and the company that built America's B-2 stealth bomber, which was intended to help drive a focus on STEM (Science, Technology, Engineering and Math) subjects for younger readers, while certainly buying Northrop some good press and shining a light on Marvel's comic books.

While Northrop Grumman doesn't only trade on defense contracts, they were worth an estimated $20 billion in profits for fiscal year 2016 alone, drawing comparisons from many on social media to "Stark Industries," which according to Marvel lore, saw a transition *away* from producing weapons once Tony Stark realized how much suffering his work had caused the world. Of course, the irony that Stark continues to fly around the world in a weaponized, bullet proof suit, or that he equips the Avengers, Shield, and teenage kids with powerful weapon systems inside the comic world they're defending, seemed lost to many of those complaining.

Nonetheless, the backlash proved effective, as Marvel rapidly announced that they would be ending the partnership they had just begun, and in even more dramatic fashion, they canceled it just before a scheduled joint event at New York Comic Con.

"The activation with Northrop Grumman at New York Comic Con was meant to focus on aerospace technology and exploration in a positive way. However, as the spirit of that intent has not come across, we will not be proceeding with this partnership including this weekend's event programming. Marvel and Northrop Grumman continue to be committed to elevating, and introducing, STEM to a broad audience." Marvel wrote in an official statement.[87]

One could argue that this is a great example of how quickly companies can respond to an outpouring of rejection from their fan base, and if that was what had happened, it would make sense. The thing is, to people who have been *reading* comic books, the outrage seems just a little out-of-place. Anyone who picked up a comic book in the nineties will likely recall the combination of giant muscles, giant breasts, and even bigger guns that covered every page. The X-Men's famed "Blackbird" jet is clearly a modified SR-71. Hell, one of the X-Men (Kitty Pride) used to fly in that SR-71 with her pet dragon named "*Lockheed*" for a while.

Comics and warfare are nothing new, just ask Captain America, so it seems far more likely that the response on social media came less from actual comic book *readers*, and more from the ever-growing number of people who spend their free time jumping on the bandwagon of whatever social media outrage is trending this week. After all, what could be worse than featuring Northrop Grumman infused science into a medium already famous for its depictions of brutal physical combat, domestic violence, and murder, just to name a few. If anything, a three-page reprieve, in which the scantily clad superheroines talk aerodynamics instead of doing airborne splits, would probably tone down the violence depicted in the book.

Politics aren't a new thing for comic books either, as many comics, including Marvel's Luke Cage that went on to become a hit show, have focused on progressive themes all along. In many ways, the creative process and the marketing strategy behind Marvel Comics, and their decision to partner with companies like Northrop, are the same as they ever were ... it's their response to the backlash that's new.

"The backlash against Marvel's planned project with Northrop Grumman was immediate and I have never seen them reverse themselves — or do anything, for that matter—as fast as they just did." Jesse Farrell, a retailer with the Massachusetts-based Hub Comics, said.[88] He's not wrong. Marvel's immediate willingness to kick Northrop Grumman to the curb as soon as they became a trending topic depicts a shift in strategy toward simply yielding to public outcry.

What does that mean for the big picture? It seems likely that Marvel's fear of public reprisal will result in further limiting of the content within the comics, as decided by those who never purchase or read them, and eventually, this may contribute to the end of the printed medium for stories about our favorite heroes all together. As a comic book reader would likely try to argue, *good stories and good artwork* sell comic books, not trying to stay right with Twitter.

Propaganda and Comic Books: An objective analysis of the US Army Cyber Command's new 'Threatcasting' publications

Anytime Russian influence campaigns are addressed in an article, you can count on two comments popping up in short order. The first will be from an old timer that doesn't believe perceptions can be managed through the digital sphere, so they'd prefer to keep their head planted firmly in the sand, and the second is from the geopolitically righteous youngin' that wants to make sure we constantly acknowledge that the United States has done its fair share of meddling too.

Our contemporary interest in the ways governments manipulate people both within and beyond their borders, of course, is often short sighted. As SOFREP contributor and Psychological Operations expert Salil Puri points out, "*influence* is the function of every nation's perception management efforts, and the digital realm is merely the newest platform utilized to that end."

From an objective standpoint, the Russian government has has some success in this realm, but don't let the headlines fool you. Being *good* at influence campaigns means utilizing a layered approach that achieves multiple objectives simultaneously, allowing you to misdirect questions about intent with answers about unrelated results. For a case study in this method of manipulation, we don't need to peruse leaflets blowing around Red Square in Moscow. In fact, we need look no further than the United States Army's Cyber Command, and the new promotional comic books being released as a part of their ongoing "Threatcasting" endeavor in conjunction with West Point Academy and Arizona State University.

Their first releases, entitled, "Silent Run" and "Dark Hammer," depict near future conflicts with Russia and North Korea, both of which find the United States operating at a distinct disadvantage.

"Silent Run" shows Russian forces utilizing a cyber attack against NATO assets on Europe's Eastern flank, allowing Russian troops to invade Romania, a legitimate concern since the Russian annexation of Crimea in 2014. The comic's depiction of events, written by futurist Brian David Johnson but informed by members of the Army's Cyber Command, could easily become a reality ... but they could also be called something else from an analytical perspective: fear mongering.

That's the up close and personal shot the comic gives us of American troops being killed by the unstoppable Russian advance, bolstered by their ability to cripple or gain control of different elements of the U.S. military's digital infrastructure – the potential future Cyber Command is tasked with preventing. It doesn't get better from there.

Not a happy ending for Romania.

"Dark Hammer," by comparison, presents a slightly rosier image of the American military's future, in that they win the battle against a superior North Korean invasion force that has already pushed U.S. and South Korean troops back into Seoul, and of course, destroyed the USS Ronald Reagan.

The U.S. Commander on the ground is faced with a seemingly impossible predicament: send his infantry troops in to face off with the superior North Korean force, or attempt to take out their command and control element with artillery, which would be sure to kill civilians and compromise the locations of their assets. Finally, the commander decides to send one of the story's two protagonists, a female Infantry platoon leader, and her soldiers into a fight they may not win... only to be stopped by the unit's Cyber Planner, who says they've been authorized to use their digital secret weapon even the battalion commander appears to be unaware of: Dark Hammer.

The "Dark Hammer," it turns out, is a secret cyber attack capability that allows the U.S. troops to completely cripple North Korea's communications, "turning their own artillery against themselves, and destroying their autonomous forces."

The comic doesn't address how North Korea's autonomous forces have become such a looming threat in the next nine years, nor does it explain how decades old artillery assets could be "turned" against North Korea through a cyber attack, but comic books are allotted some leeway when it comes to realism.

Thanks to the capabilities allotted by U.S. Cyber Command, disaster is averted and the underdog United States lives to fight another day against the seemingly superior North Korean offensive.

So what's at play in these comic books? They were clearly released with intent, but before an analysis of what that intent may be, it's important to address our perceptions of loaded words like *intent, manipulation, perception, and propaganda.* In many contexts, each of those words carries a distinctly negative connotation. Russia's *intent* was to *manipulate* the American people's *perceptions* through *propaganda.* However, from the (seemingly cynical) perspective of people who study this sort of thing, nearly *all* content distributed through media of *any* sort has the *intent* of *manipulating perceptions.* Marketing is private sector propaganda, aimed at informing your purchases. Public relations is, again, private sector propaganda, aimed at managing your perceptions of companies or individuals. Even the dreaded "click bait" is a modern form of of the same influence... pushing you to click on a link, because clicks are the currency of the digital realm.

That's a long way of saying, just because a piece of content has the intent to manipulate you, doesn't make it inherently nefarious. It's just the way of the world, for better or worse.

As discussed previously, effective propaganda is delivered in a layered approach, fulfilling the needs or accomplishing the objectives of multiple efforts as a means of not only plausible deniability, but to ensure the content is well received by an increasingly cynical audience in the era of "fake news" accusations and pervasive marketing. For propaganda to be effective, it's got to be the cream filling, not the Oreo cookie exterior. With that in mind, three distinct perception management campaigns are evident in these two comic books released by the U.S. Army.

Recruitment

While one might think that two comic books that depict U.S. forces losing, or very nearly losing battles against enemies like Russia or North Korea wouldn't serve as a powerful recruitment aid, many who have served might tell you differently. These comics depict American forces as the underdog in a fight not only for their lives, but to protect the people of South Korea and Romania against the ever-nefarious "other" – represented in these instances by foreign nations that are currently no more than diplomatic opponents of the United States.

For many red-blooded Americans, these depictions of individual heroes (notably a female hero in one of the stories) willing to put their lives on the line to defend those in need is exactly the sort of thing they hope to do when signing on the dotted line. These stories advance the *perception* that serving in the American military is your chance to *make a difference.*

All materials produced by the Department of Defense for media consumption, it pays to remember, has some element of recruiting involved.

Managing Perceptions of American Opponents

The U.S. Army usually doesn't identify the names of the nations they're training to only potentially fight. That's why fictional nations like Atropia were invented – to ensure the Army's training doesn't have a negative effect on international relations... it's hard to enter into high level talks with a nation like Russia aimed at diffusing tensions, while simultaneously conducting "Operation Get Ready to Invade Moscow" at Fort Benning. As such, *real* potential opponents' names are often left out of hypothetical conflicts... but that's not the case in Cyber Command's "Threatcasting" comics.

By directly identifying Russia and North Korea as the aggressors in both instances, these comics are making intentional choices about how the reader perceives them. Both comics open by providing some character development to their U.S. troops, either through banter or flashbacks to their all-American childhoods, playing football in the backyard. The enemy forces, on the other hand, remain completely faceless throughout, and with good reason. Just like the Stormtroopers in Star Wars, the Borg in Star Trek, zombies in the Walking Dead and the ninja Foot Clan in Teenage Mutant Ninja Turtles, robbing an opponent of their individuality, of their identity, also robs them of their humanity. We can hack at zombies and blast away at Stormtroopers because they *aren't people* to us. They're the nameless, faceless *them* we all fear.

Showing the aggression of these foreign states, but not their faces or stories, is a narrative decision that gives us, the reader, a clear protagonist to root for – but because they represent *real* nations made up of *real* people, these depictions can also skew the way we see these populations, and in turn, the possibility of conflict with them. Note, this isn't a *criticism* of the narrative, but rather an observation about the choices made in the depiction of the characters.

Internal Posturing

While the first two underlying perception management efforts depicted in these comics may be fairly easy to glean, the third requires a bit of an "insider baseball" approach. The U.S. Army's Cyber Command is an entirely new endeavor, first established only eight years ago and rapidly expanding to address the growing challenge presented in warfare's digital theater. Because of its relative youth compared to more well established command structures within the U.S.

military and the unprecedented nature of the challenges it faces, there is no established procedure for Cyber's growth.

Cyber Command's leadership, as a result, have been jockeying to absorb more authority over elements of the U.S. Defense infrastructure that tie into elements of their purview. One of these elements is on full display in the "Silent Ruin" comic, where it's Russia's ability to neutralize U.S. drones with a cyber attack that gives them the advantage. The underlying premise being, without Cyber Command's oversight, American drones are vulnerable.

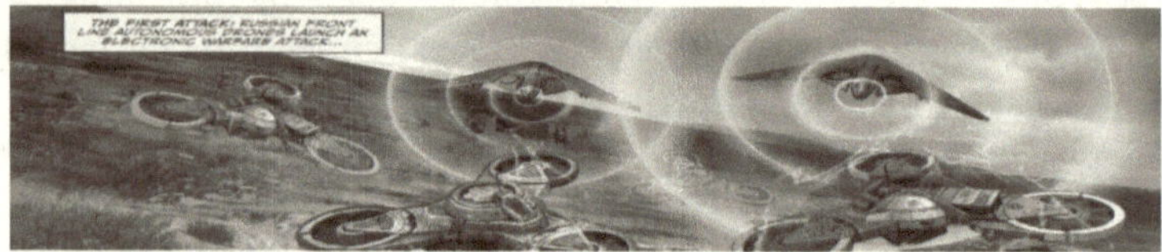

Likewise in "Dark Hammer," it's Cyber Command's development of a digital weapon that even senior ranking officers seem only passively aware of that wins the day.

In both instances, it's the U.S. Cyber Command's autonomy, and inferred budget, that holds the key to American victory.

"Every unit is competing for their piece of the budget," Salil Puri explained, "And Cyber has a history of trying to expand their domain."

Conclusion

There is no denying that perception management efforts have shaped the world we find ourselves in today, and will continue to shape the one we found ourselves in tomorrow. The endeavor, in itself, is not a nefarious one however -- it's the intent of the narrative that truly determines where a campaign falls on the spectrum of good versus evil.

One could argue that narrative played a powerful role in keeping America invested in the war effort that aided in the Allied defeat of Nazi Germany in World War II, just as one could attest that Cold War narratives helped amass public support for the Gemini and Apollo missions that stretched mankind's concepts of what we, as a species, were capable of accomplishing. The tools at many national government's disposal to frame concepts in the minds of their people and the people beyond their borders can be powerful, and when used for the wrong purposes can have significant impact on a nation's safety and prosperity... but when used to encourage an acceptance of the *truth*, perception management efforts can be the tools of noble as well as the nefarious.

As Americans grow increasingly divided along ideological lines, the nation has become more susceptible to bad actor narratives than ever before. Our distrust for the opposing party and for our government creates a fertile ground for confirmation bias driven perception strategies that can push the wedge even further between us, and to quote the Greek story tell Aesop as so many have before, *"united we stand, divided we fall."*

As media consumers, we have the power to stem the tide of malign efforts among ourselves, however. *Bias,* as we've grown to look for in journalism, exists in all forms of messaging: *look* for it, be skeptical of things that seem to fit too neatly into your preconceived beliefs. Think twice before you share something on social media that doesn't quite seem to be on the level.

Ultimately, the governments of the world will always work to find ways to change your mind... But it's still your mind.

Be careful how you make it.

THE PERCEPTION WARS

This book was published with the express permission of SOFREP's editorial staff.

By Alex Hollings

INDEX

---

[1] **7 Unbelievable Ways the Government Wasted Your Money in 2015**

http://www.thefiscaltimes.com/2015/12/22/7-Unbelievable-Ways-Government-Wasted-Your-Money-2015

[2] **Fact or Fiction?: Nasa Spent Millions To Develop a Pen That Would Write in Space, Whereas the Soviet Cosmonauts Used a Pencil**

Ciara Curtin - https://www.scientificamerican.com/article/fact-or-fiction-nasa-spen/

[3] **The Fisher Space Pen Boldly Writes Where No Man Has Written Before**

Jimmy Stamp - http://www.smithsonianmag.com/arts-culture/the-fisher-space-pen-boldly-writes-where-no-man-has-written-before-1020748/?no-ist=

[4] **Soviet Space Propaganda: Doctored Cosmonaut**

By Alex Hollings

Photos

James Oberg – https://www.wired.com/2011/04/soviet-space-propaganda/

5 Everything Worth Believing About The Lost Cosmonauts Theory

Daniel Ortberg – http://the-toast.net/2014/06/17/everything-worth-believing-lost-cosmonauts-theory/

6 Chilling Audio Of Lost Cosmonaut Inspires Short Film

Dustin Wicksell – http://www.inquisitr.com/1523310/chilling-audio-of-lost-cosmonaut-inspires-short-film/

7 Cosmonaut Crashed Into Earth 'crying In Rage'

Robert Krulwich – http://www.npr.org/sections/krulwich/2011/05/02/134597833/cosmonaut-crashed-into-earth-crying-in-rage

8 Deaths Associated with Us Space Programs

LLC AirSafe.com – http://www.airsafe.com/events/space/astrofat.htm

---

9 The Cannibal Hell Of Stalin's Prison Island

Mark Franchetti - http://www.thesundaytimes.co.uk/sto/news/world_news/article62636.ece

10 Cannibal Island

https://books.google.com/books?id=s72TevH9XOcC&pg=PA159&lpg=PA159&dq=nazino%2Baffair&source=bl&ots=sJoG7_vq7y&sig=6zl58WaP5tlFBNFk2PNYnZ_0K9Q&hl=en&sa=X&ved=0ahUKEwiOs-LCkvnQAhWITSYKHe57BYg4FBDoAQgwMAQ#v=onepage&q=nazino%20affair&f=false

11 Black book of communism: crimes, terror, repression

Stephane Courtois - Harvard Univ Press - 2015

12 Lee Harvey Oswald, Disappointed Revolutionary

Peter Savodnik - https://www.wsj.com/articles/SB10001424052702303722604579111222338096030

13 Andrew and Mitrokhin, The Sword and the Shield

http://www.jfk-online.com/mitrokhin.html

---

[14] Fears, D. (2005, January 25). Study: Many Blacks Cite AIDS Conspiracy. Retrieved from http://www.washingtonpost.com/wp-dyn/articles/A33695-2005Jan24.html

[15] Boghardt, T. (2009, December). Soviet Bloc Intelligence and Its AIDS Disinformation Campaign. Retrieved from https://www.cia.gov/library/center-for-the-study-of-intelligence/csi-publications/csi-studies/studies/vol53no4/pdf/U- Boghardt-AIDS-Made in the USA-17Dec.pdf

[16] **Intelligence in Public Literature**

https://www.cia.gov/library/center-for-the-study-of-intelligence/csi-publications/csi-studies/studies/vol-58-no-4/russian-roulette-how-british-spies-thwarted-lenin2019s-plot-for-global-revolution.html

[17] **British Spy 'fired the Shot That Finished Off Rasputin'**

Karyn Miller - http://www.telegraph.co.uk/education/3344528/British-spy-fired-the-shot-that-finished-off-Rasputin.html

[18] **British Spy's Link To Murder Of Rasputin**

Ben Macintyre -

---

http://www.thetimes.co.uk/article/british-spys-link-to-murder-of-rasputin-6bfd6ng6s

[19] Little Evidence Of Health Benefits from Organic Foods, Stanford Study Finds

News Center - https://med.stanford.edu/news/all-news/2012/09/little-evidence-of-health-benefits-from-organic-foods-study-finds.html

[20] While Warning About Fat, U.s. Pushes Cheese Sales

Michael Moss - http://www.nytimes.com/2010/11/07/us/07fat.html

[21] A Wwii Propaganda Campaign Popularized the Myth That Carrots Help You See in the Dark

K. Smith - https://www.smithsonianmag.com/arts-culture/a-wwii-propaganda-campaign-popularized-the-myth-that-carrots-help-you-see-in-the-dark-28812484/

[22] Report of the APA Task Force on Advertising and Children. (n.d.). Retrieved from http://www.apa.org/pubs/info/reports/advertising-children.aspx

[23] Fake Russian Facebook Accounts Bought $100,000 in Political Ads

---

Scott Shane-Vindu Goel -
https://www.nytimes.com/2017/09/06/technology/fa
cebook-russian-political-ads.html

24 Jackie Chan Tempers Anti-u.s. Rhetoric Long Enough To Sell You Tickets To His New Movie

Alex Hollings - https://sofrep.com/84504/jackie-
chan-tempers-anti-u-s-rhetoric-long-enough-
sell-tickets-new-movie/

25 The Website For the Embassy Of the Russian Federation in the Usa Has Moved

http://www.russianembassy.org/article/comment-
by-foreign-ministry-spokesperson-maria-
zakharova-following-the-latest-expansion-of-u

26 Russian Tank Maker Publishes 'patriotic' Children's Book

News Elsewhere... -
http://www.bbc.com/news/blogs-news-from-
elsewhere-38770226

27 Would You Read the Story Of "the Little Tank" By Russia's Arms Maker?

Damien Sharkov -
http://www.newsweek.com/russias-tank-maker-
published-childrens-book-full-patriotism-548653

[28] **A Russian Company Is Selling Children's Beds Resembling the Missile Launcher That Downed Mh17**

David Filipov - https://www.washingtonpost.com/news/worldviews/ wp/2016/10/04/a-russian-company-is-selling- childrens-beds-modeled-after-the-missile- launcher-that-downed- mh17/?utm_term=.4bf49fe2f356

[29] **Russia To Limp Bizkit's Fred Durst: You'll Always Have a Home in Crimea**

Siobhán O'Grady - http://foreignpolicy.com/2015/10/08/russia-to-limp- bizkits-fred-durst-youll-always-have-a-home-in- crimea/

[30] **Limp Bizkit Vocalist Fred Durst Wants To Become Russian Citizen**

Sputnik - https://sputniknews.com/art_living/20150901102645 9347-limp-bizkit-russian-citizen/

[31] **Fred Durst Wants To Make Films For the 'great Future' Of Russia and Annexed Crimea**

Vladimir Kozlov - http://www.billboard.com/articles/business/6722889

/fred-durst-films-russia-crimea

32 Limp Bizkit's Fred Durst Banned By Ukrainian Government: Reports

Associated Press - http://www.billboard.com/articles/columns/rock/681 4192/limp-bizkit-fred-durst-banned-ukraine

33 White House: Russia, Syrian Regime Trying To 'confuse' the World Over Chemical Attacks

Jeff Zeleny-Dan Merica - http://www.cnn.com/2017/04/11/politics/white-house-russia-syria-chemical-weapons/index.html

34 Putin Says Expects 'fake' Gas Attacks To Discredit Syria's Assad

http://www.reuters.com/article/us-mideast-crisis-syria-usa-putin-idUSKBN17D1K9

35 White House Says Russia Increasingly Isolated Over Syria

Steve Holland - http://www.reuters.com/article/us-mideast-crisis-syria-usa-whitehouse-idUSKBN17D25Q

36 Pepsi Pulls Ad Accused Of Trivializing Black Lives Matter

Daniel Victor -
https://www.nytimes.com/2017/04/05/business/kend
all-jenner-pepsi-ad.html

37 Russia Accuses U.s. Of Pretending To Fight Islamic State in Syria,...

http://www.reuters.com/article/us-mideast-crisis-
syria-russia-usa/russia-accuses-u-s-of-
pretending-to-fight-islamic-state-in-syria-iraq-
idUSKBN1CF0KN

38 Airstrike Updates. (n.d.). Retrieved from
https://www.defense.gov/OIR/Airstrikes/?Page=4

39 Russia Offers Bogus "evidence" That U.s. Is Helping Isis

Tucker Reals -
https://www.cbsnews.com/news/russia-video-
game-evidence-us-direct-cooperation-support-
isis-syria-raqqa/

40 Raqqa's Dirty Secret - Bbc News

http://www.bbc.co.uk/news/resources/idt-
sh/raqqas_dirty_secret

41 Russia Tried To Use Computer-game Footage To Prove That the U.s. Is Helping Isis

---

Damien Sharkov -
http://www.newsweek.com/russias-evidence-us-helping-isis-comes-2015-computer-game-710474

42 Russian Su-35 Chased Away Rogue Us F-22 Jet: Mod Blasts Us Air Force For Hampering Syria Op

https://www.rt.com/news/412590-russia-us-syria-air-force/

43 A Russian Su-35 Allegedly Chased Away an F-22 Over Syria

David Cenciotti -
http://www.businessinsider.com/russian-su-35-allegedly-chased-away-f-22-over-syria-2017-12

44 Russians Already Meddling in Us Midterms, Tillerson Says

Rich Edson -
http://www.foxnews.com/politics/2018/02/06/russians-already-meddling-in-us-midterms-tillerson-says.html

45 Russian Trolls Created Facebook Events Seen By More Than 300,000 Users

On occasions -
http://money.cnn.com/2018/01/26/media/russia-trolls-facebook-events/index.html

46 **Associated Press News**

http://hosted.ap.org/dynamic/stories/A/APFN_US_R
USSIAN_HACKERS_CONTRACTORS?SITE=AP&SECTI
ON=HOME&TEMPLATE=DEFAULT

47 **China Extends Hollywood Push with $1 Billion Paramount Investment**

Jessica Toonkel - http://www.reuters.com/article/us-
viacom-paramount-china-idUSKBN153335

48 **How China's Censors Influence Hollywood**

Frank Langfitt -
http://www.npr.org/sections/parallels/2015/05/18/40
7619652/how-chinas-censors-influence-hollywood

49 **15 Movies That Made Drastic Changes For A Chinese Audience**

Matthew Loffhagen - http://screenrant.com/movies-
changed-for-china/?view=al

50 **Caucasian Female Body Hair and American Culture**

Christine Hope -
http://onlinelibrary.wiley.com/doi/10.1111/j.1542-
734X.1982.0501_93.x/abstract

---

51 We Buy Engagement Rings Because a Diamond Company Wanted Us To

Uri Friedman - http://www.theatlantic.com/international/archive/2015/02/how-an-ad-campaign-invented-the-diamond-engagement-ring/385376/

52 Color ordered: a survey of color systems from antiquity to the present

Rolf Kuehni-Andreas Schwarz - Oxford University Press - 2008

53 No One Could See the Colour Blue Until Modern Times

Kevin Loria - http://www.businessinsider.com.au/what-is-blue-and-how-do-we-see-color-2015-2

54 Summer the Chinese Spy and the Hazards Of the Shot Show

Jack Murphy- Army Special Operations- 5th Special Forces Group. - https://sofrep.com/46331/summer-the-chinese-spy-and-the-hazards-of-the-shot-show/

55 Beijing Offers Cash Rewards To Unearth Foreign Spies

http://www.reuters.com/article/us-china-security-idUSKBN17C09S

56 **To Catch a Spy: Beijing Offers $70,000 Reward - and a Cartoon Video To Help in the Hunt**

Simon Denyer - https://www.washingtonpost.com/news/worldviews/wp/2017/04/10/to-catch-a-spy-beijing-offers-70000-reward-and-a-cartoon-video-to-help-in-the-hunt/?utm_term=.7a5e0f3bf03d

57 **Beijing Offers Hefty Cash Reward For Spy Tip-offs**

http://www.bbc.com/news/world-asia-china-39550673

58 **Oops! Chinese Defence Ministry's Big Photoshop Fail**

http://www.scmp.com/news/china/diplomacy-defence/article/2090448/oops-chinese-defence-ministrys-pla-poster-big-photoshop

59 **The J-20: China's Counterfeit-fighter That Could Still Mean Trouble**

Alex Hollings - https://sofrep.com/67488/j-20-chinas-counterfeit-fighter-still-mean-trouble/

60 **Defense Ministry Apologies For Poster Error**

蔺丽瑶 - http://www.china.org.cn/china/2017-04/28/content_40711712.htm

[61] **Jackie Chan To America: 'it's Not Me. It's You.'**

Benjamin Carlson - http://www.cnbc.com/id/100389754

[62] **The Anti-americanism Of Jackie Chan**

Max Fisher - https://www.washingtonpost.com/news/worldviews/wp/2013/01/10/the-anti-americanism-of-jackie-chan/?utm_term=.b3ad7eb0c611

[63] **Jackie Chan 'worried' That Protests Are Harming Hong Kong's Finances**

Elizabeth Barber - http://time.com/3488836/jackie-chan-worried-pro-democracy-protests-harm-hong-kongs-finances/

[64] **Kung Fu Star Jackie Chan Appointed To Top China Communist Party Committee**

Umberto Bacchi - http://www.ibtimes.co.uk/jackie-chan-communist-430569

[65] **Jackie Chan: 'warcraft' Success in China "scares the Americans"**

THR Staff - http://www.hollywoodreporter.com/news/jackie-chan-warcraft-success-china-901868

66 **Indian Character in Jackie Chan Movie Used For Pro-china 'propaganda'**

http://www.hindustantimes.com/world-news/indian-character-in-jackie-chan-movie-used-for-pro-china-propaganda/story-FRl027f80j3VSbBYWOeE3K.htm

67 **A Bunch Of American Box-office Flops Were Global Hits In 2016**

Dustin Rowles - http://uproxx.com/movies/american-box-office-bombs-internationally/5/

68 **China Orders Propaganda Videos At Movie Screenings**

Kevin Lui - http://time.com/4848569/china-theaters-propaganda-movies-cinema/#

69 **Viral Chinese Video Game Measures Which Players Can Clap Fastest For President Xi Jinping**

Cheang Ming - https://www.cnbc.com/2017/10/19/tencent-game-users-clap-chinese-president-xi-jinping-party-congress-speech.html

70 North Korea's Birthday Celebrations Included Fake Video Of Missile Strikes on Us

http://www.abc.net.au/news/2017-04-19/north-korea-airs-mock-up-video-of-missiles-striking-us/8455114

71 The Assassination Of Kim Jong Nam Was Almost Certainly Ordered By North Korea's Supreme Leader

Alex Hollings - https://sofrep.com/74824/the-assassination-of-kim-jong-nam-was-almost-certainly-ordered-by-north-koreas-supreme-leader/

72 Rodman Hopes To Do 'something Pretty Positive' in North Korea

Matt Rivers-Will Ripley-Joshua Berlinger - http://www.cnn.com/2017/06/13/politics/dennis-rodman-north-korea/index.html

73 North Korea Rejects Diplomacy with Us For Now, Source Says

Will Ripley-Zachary Cohen-Richard Roth - http://www.cnn.com/2017/10/16/politics/north-korea-negotiations-trump-tillerson/index.html

74 North Korea Missile Test Puts Major Us Cities in Range, Experts Say

Brad Lendon - http://www.cnn.com/2017/07/29/asia/north-korea-intercontinental-ballistic-missile-test/index.html

75 North Korea: Missile Can Reach Entire Continental U.s.

Heesu Kong - http://time.com/4879527/kim-jong-un-north-korea-missile-could-strike-entire-continental-u-s/

76 North Korea Has Threatened a U.s. Attack For Years. Why Aren't You Scared?

Adam Taylor - https://www.washingtonpost.com/news/worldviews/wp/2015/08/17/north-korea-has-threatened-a-u-s-attack-for-years-why-arent-you-scared/?utm_term=.d6516c81722a

77 North Korean Photo Reveals 'u.s. Mainland Strike Plan'

James Pearson - https://www.nknews.org/2013/03/breaking-north-korean-photo-reveals-u-s-mainland-strike-plan/

**78 North Korea Threatens 'pre-emptive' Nuclear

Strike

http://www.abc.net.au/news/2013-03-07/north-korea-threatens-27pre-emptive27-nuclear-strike/4559532

[79] **North Korea Threatens Us With 'final Doom'**

Sky News - http://news.sky.com/story/north-korea-threatens-us-with-final-doom-10372732

[80] **Putin on North Korea's Missile Test: 'no Threat To Us.' Jabs At U.s. Foreign Policy**

Alex Hollings - https://sofrep.com/81342/putin-north-koreas-missile-test-no-threat-us-jabs-u-s-foreign-policy/

[81] **North Korea Accuses the Cia and South Korea Of 'biochemical' Assassination Plot Aimed At Kim Jong Un**

Alex Hollings - https://sofrep.com/80679/north-korea-accuses-cia-south-korea-biochemical-assassination-plot-aimed-kim-jong-un/

[82] **New Ferry Service Links Russia- North Korea Despite International Calls To Isolate Kim Regime**

Alex Hollings - https://sofrep.com/81692/new-ferry-service-links-russia-north-korea-despite-international-calls-isolate-kim-regime/

83 **Fake Russian Facebook Accounts Bought $100,000 in Political Ads**

Scott Shane-Vindu Goel - https://www.nytimes.com/2017/09/06/technology/facebook-russian-political-ads.html

84 **A Cold War Conundrum: The 1983 Soviet War Scare**

https://www.cia.gov/library/center-for-the-study-of-intelligence/csi-publications/books-and-monographs/a-cold-war-conundrum/source.htm#HEADING1-07

85 **B-52 Testers Complete Leaflet Bomb Drops**

http://www.edwards.af.mil/News/Article/1257229/b-52-testers-complete-leaflet-bomb-drops/

86 **Comic Book Sales By Month**

http://www.comichron.com/monthlycomicssales.html

87 **Marvel Cancels Comic Crossover with Defense Giant Northrop Grumman [updated]**

Beth Elderkin - https://io9.gizmodo.com/marvel-cancels-nycc-event-for-comic-crossover-with-defe-1819242675

---

[88] What Just Happened with Northrop and Marvel Comics?

Aaron Mehta –
https://www.defensenews.com/industry/2017/10/07/
what-just-happened-with-northrop-and-marvel-
comics-analysis/